BRUNO P⌐

ALGY
THE PRIVILEGED LIFE OF TITANIC
SURVIVOR ALGERNON BARKWORTH

FOREWORD BY RANDY BRYAN BIGHAM AND GREGG JASPER

Book Layout – **Rafaela Pedigoni Mauro**
Cover Art and Design – **Tatiana Yamshanova**
Picture Editing – **Randy Bryan Bigham**
Publisher – **Amazon**

Dados Internacionais de Catalogação na Publicação (CIP) (Câmara Brasileira do Livro, SP, Brasil)

Piola, Bruno
  Algy : the privileged life of titanic survivor
Algernon Barkworth / Bruno Piola. -- 1. ed. --
Franca, SP : Ed. do Autor, 2022.
  ISBN 978-65-00-44329-5
  1. Barkworth, Algernon Henry, 1864-1945
2. Homens - Biografia 3. Sobreviventes 4. Titanic
(Navio a vapor) - História I. Título.

22-109613   CDD-920.71

Índices para catálogo sistemático:

1. Homens : Biografia 920.71
Aline Graziele Benitez - Bibliotecária - CRB-1/3129

*To Justin Lowe and Michael
Free, whose research and friendship
made this book a reality*

Summary

Foreword

By *Randy Bryan Bigham*
and Gregg Jasper

Algernon 'Algy' Barkworth wasn't a celebrity nor had he any ambitions to be. He was a well-educated, prosperous British landowner who found his calling as a civil servant and philanthropist. Algy's extraordinary survival of the sinking of Titanic propelled him into fame although he did not court the attention that came his way. Instead, he continued to pursue a relatively quiet, though illustrious, life of public service and charitable work.

Personally, Algy was fastidious, outgoing socially, well-spoken, witty and loyal to his friends and family. He was also gay, but despite the prejudices of his era, he maintained a high profile in his community, both among his peers and his neighbors.

His story has not been told in full detail until now. Bruno Piola, who has previously written the first book on the Brazilian connections to the Titanic disaster, *Faces do Titanic* ('Faces of the Titanic'), as well as contributed articles to Voyage, the journal of Titanic International Society, has applied his skills as a journalist to telling the truth about Algy Barkworth's memorable life and career. Enlisting Barkworth's family and the descendants of others who knew him, Piola has networked with fellow historians to amass many personal accounts and never-before-seen photos, ultimately penning a definitive biography.

In these pages, Piola has beautifully presented the story of an incredible man who achieved much professionally, survived an epic catastrophe and led an unconventional private life with bravery and dignity.

Randy Bryan Bigham and Gregg Jasper are writers, historians and Titanic *researchers. Together, they have written articles and the book* Broadway Dame - The Life and Times of Mrs. Henry B. Harris, *a biography of* Titanic *survivor Renée Harris.*

Introduction

I was not planning to write this book. Not as it is now, anyway.

I published my first book, *Faces do Titanic* ('Faces of the Titanic'), written in Portuguese in April 2020, after working on it for two and a half years. It tells the stories of several *Titanic* passengers and crew members while unravelling the several connections the ship has to my home country, Brazil. It is over 400 pages and, after it was done, I felt really proud but exhausted, too. That's why I took the rest of the year off from writing.

The next opportunity to write a book appeared in early 2021. It was going to be a work about the people aboard the *Titanic* who were a part of what is today called the LGBTQIA+ community. Again, this proved to be a challenge, but I was going to write it with two other authors, my friends Gregg Jasper and Randy Bryan Bigham. Plans for this work eventually fell through, much to my and my co-authors' regret. However, some good things came out of it. Randy and Gregg wrote a beautiful article about *Titanic* survivor Marion Becker that will be published soon in *Voyage*, the Titanic International Society's journal. And I had an almost-finished chapter on Algernon Barkworth for the planned book.

Although our goal was to discuss these people's sexual orientation, perhaps for the first time in print, we also wanted to write about their lives as a whole. Who were they, really? What did they think of life? What were their interests and fears? My take on what was supposed to be a 'mini-biography' of Barkworth turned out to be bigger than I ever expected. He lived a very long life and, being an active member of his community in East Yorkshire, England, it was well documented in newspapers. I was also lucky that I managed to contact several researchers who were successful in uncovering new information on him throughout the years and were kind enough to share their discoveries with me. I dedicate this book to two of them.

Because of the amount of material I have gathered, including some never-before-seen pictures, I found myself with a manuscript longer than an article or a chapter. I then decided to publish my work as a book in order to tell Algernon's story in full. He is a fascinating character whose survival of the *Titanic* tragedy was incredible, to say the least. But aside from that, his life was so full of nuances, interesting events and controversies that I feel that he deserves to be known as more than a *Titanic* survivor. I hope you agree with me when you finish reading this book.

Welcome aboard!
Bruno Piola, 19 December 2021

CHAPTER 1

'Everything is most magnificent'

As the *Titanic* was gliding through the frigid waters of the North Atlantic Ocean late at night on 14 April 1912, already in the ice field that would soon seal her fate, 47-year-old British Justice of the Peace Algernon Henry Barkworth was enjoying the warmth of the ship's First Class Smoking Room.

His trip had been delightful up to that point. A wealthy citizen from a small town called Hessle in East Yorkshire, Algernon had decided to visit the United States partly to see how it would be to sail on the biggest liner in the world. Although a seasoned traveller, this would be his first trip to America, and Barkworth planned to stay there for a month on vacation. His trip on the *Titanic* was meant to be just another chapter in his carefree, privileged life. His First Class ticket alone had cost 30 pounds, which today would be the equivalent of £3,037.[1]

---

1. *Scarborough Mercury*, 19 April 1912; *Evening Banner*, 26 April 1912; Encyclopedia Titanica (Link: https://www.encyclopedia-titanica.org/titanic-survivor/algernon-barkworth.html). Visited on 12 February 2022; MeasuringWorth.Com (Link: https://www.measuringworth.com/calculators/ppoweruk/). This and all the subsequent inflation calculations for this book were made in December 2021.

His first days aboard the White Star liner are well documented thanks mainly to a few postcards and cablegrams Algernon sent to family and acquaintances, starting on 10 April, when he embarked at Southampton. On that day, his message to his brother Edmund revealed his amazement at the *Titanic*'s luxuriousness. 'Have made a good start and are nearing Cherbourg [the ship's first port of call]. Everything is <u>most</u> [his emphasis] magnificent and impossible to describe', he said. For a newspaper, Barkworth would also recall how 'the magnificence of the appointments of the liner' made a lasting impression on him.[2]

Around 6.30 p.m., as the *Titanic* was arriving in the French coastal city, Algernon penned another note, this time to his niece Dorothy, Edmund's daughter, of whom he was quite fond. 'Rather stormy and cold but in my room you would hardly know the engines were going', he wrote.[3] His cabin was A-23, on the starboard side of the *Titanic*'s A Deck, and indeed no more than nine decks separated his berth from the base of the ship's two gigantic reciprocating engines and her low-pressure turbine (which drove the central propeller using waste steam from the engines). Given its ideal location, A Deck was exclusive to First Class passengers like Barkworth.

---

2. *Daily Mail*, 17 May 1912.

3. Edwards, Brian, *A Swim for Dear Life – The True Story of a Titanic Survivor*, page 9. Courtesy of Bruce Robinson.

Algernon Barkworth ca. the 1910s – this is his best-known photograph (Justin Lowe Collection)

The Titanic arriving at Cherbourg Harbour: 'Have made a good start and are nearing Cherbourg. Everything is most

magnificent and impossible to describe', wrote Algernon (Wikimedia Commons)

On the next day, the *Titanic* reached Queenstown (now Cobh), in Ireland, her last stop before New York. This allowed Algernon to write another postcard, this time to the firm that booked for him his ticket on the liner. In it, the Englishman said he had a comfortable berth.[4] His room, although small, was indeed very cosy: it contained a brass bed with a luggage rack above, a washbasin, a mahogany dressing table and chair, a wardrobe equipped with dress hangers and enclosed by a mirrored door, an electric heater for the cold nights, and a sofa berth, which could be converted into an extra bed if necessary. Most A Deck cabins also boasted portable electric fans.

His pleasant time aboard apparently continued for the next few days; he sent a cable to his mother, Catherine, through the *Titanic*'s wireless office, saying all was well. He signed the message with his family diminutive – Algy.[5]

Barkworth's social life aboard was also busy. He had met several prominent passengers during the transatlantic crossing, including the Second Vice-President of the Pennsylvania Railroad, John Borland Thayer and his son Jack, whom Algy described as a 'clean-

---

4. *Hull Daily Mail*, 15 April 1912.

5. His diminutive was said to be 'Algie' by newspapers, but a wireless message and letters written by Barkworth indeed prove the correct spelling is 'Algy'.

This cabin on the Olympic (Titanic's sister ship) gives a good idea what Algernon's cabin was like. However, his being an interior room, it would not have had a window like this one (The Shipbuilder / Courtesy of Bruce Beveridge)

The Titanic is photographed leaving Queenstown; on that day, Algernon wrote that he had gotten a comfortable berth on the liner (Wikimedia Commons)

cut chap', and the American managing director of an oil company in London, Howard Case.

Nonetheless, it was with Briton Arthur Gee and American Charles Cresson Jones that Algy spent most of his time. Whereas the former was travelling on the *Titanic* to take up a managing position in a linen mill at Atlixco, near Mexico City, the latter was coming home to resume his position as superintendent on a 4,000-acre farm in Bennington, Vermont. Jones had visited England for the purpose of buying sheep and, curiously, attended a livestock sale at Edmund Barkworth's property in the village of Piddletrenthide, in Dorset County, a few days before his trip back to the United States.[6] There is no evidence Jones and Algy had ever met before embarking on the ship,[7] but their relationship aboard was close enough to include some humorous moments. 'I think he had once lived in England for he could imitate the Dorset shepherds to perfection', joked Barkworth afterwards.[8] The trio was practically the same age, and Algernon later described the two men as 'two most agreeable chaps' and even his 'best friends'.[9]

---

6. Mowbray, Jay, *Sinking of the Titanic: Thrilling Stories Told by Survivors*, page 183; Unknown Newspaper, April 1912, courtesy of Philip Hind.

7. Indeed, Algy said to *The Sun* newspaper that he had made the 'acquaintance' of Jones and Gee coming over to the United States, which points to them all meeting on the *Titanic* for the first time.

8. Jones was living in Vermont, USA, at the time of his voyage on the *Titanic* and it is highly unlikely he ever lived in England.

9. *Evening Banner*, 26 April 1912; Account dictated to *Carpathia* passenger Mr Cecil R. Francis.

Algernon's shipboard acquaintances, from left to right: John Borland Thayer; his son, 'clean-cut' Jack; and Howard Case (Left and Centre: Wikimedia Commons; Right: Günter Bäbler Collection)

'Two most agreeable chaps': Arthur Gee (left) and Charles Cresson Jones were Algy's two best friends aboard the Titanic (Left: Martin Gee Collection; Right: Author's Collection)

The Justice of the Peace (JP) was spending his evening with Gee and Jones in the *Titanic*'s Smoking Room on 14 April. The conversation revolved around good road building – a subject Barkworth was interested in, probably because he was a car enthusiast. When Algy announced that he was going to retire to his cabin, someone informed him that the room's clock was going to be set back at midnight, and so he decided to stay to adjust his personal watch. Clock adjustments were necessary on transatlantic crossings so that the ship's time would progressively get closer to the time kept at the destination port.

Time after Time

That 'someone' who instructed Algernon about the time change must have been a passenger rather than a crew member, such as a steward, because he clearly had no knowledge of how the clocks were adjusted on the ship. The Titanic used a system of Magneta clocks that consisted of two primary clocks located in the chart room and 48 secondary clocks controlled by them. The secondary clocks could be found throughout the ship, including in the First Class Smoking Room.

On westbound journeys, like the one the Titanic was carrying out, the primary clock would be put back in time so that, at local apparent noon (the time when the sun reaches its highest altitude in the sky), the ship's clocks would read 12 o'clock. Those adjustments, as mentioned in

Barkworth's account, happened at midnight on White Star Line vessels. However, once the time change was made on the primary clocks, the secondary clocks would not go back automatically as we would assume. Actually, they would stay motionless until the primary clock caught up to the time shown on the secondary clocks.

So, on the night of 14 April 1912, the primary clocks would be put back by 23 minutes at around midnight, showing 11.37 p.m. For the next 23 minutes, the secondary clock showing midnight in the Smoking Room would have remained still until the primary clocks reached the midnight timeframe as well. Then, both primary and secondary clocks would keep up the same time. That is why it would not have done Algernon any good to stay in the smoking room and watch a frozen clock. Besides, that information would have been available in several strategic places for the passengers to alter their timepieces.

For more on how the clock system worked on the Titanic, please refer to Strangers on the Horizon: Titanic and Californian – A Forensic Approach, by Samuel Halpern.

Alas, the midnight adjustment was never performed by the crew because at around 11.40 p.m., the *Titanic* collided with an iceberg on her starboard side, breaching at least six of her watertight compartments and thus dooming her – she could float with her first four compartments flooded but no more than that. The impact stopped any roadbuilding talk for Algy and his companions. 'We heard a grinding sound which caused the ship to tremble. [The] Engines seemed to stop', he would remember later. The noise made Barkworth fearful, but neither he nor anyone else in the room panicked.

The JP decided to check out what the problem was. He exited the Smoking Room through revolving doors that gave access to the ship's Verandah Café (also called Palm Court) and, from there, went out on deck. The first person he saw was journalist W. T. Stead, who informed him that 'an iceberg had ground against the starboard side' - possibly Stead's last recorded words. Algy, however, saw nothing.

Barkworth was close to the stern of the ship, where there was no damage in sight, so he decided to go forward, in the direction of the *Titanic*'s bow. When he finally got there, Algy noticed the ship's forecastle deck covered with pieces of ice which had fallen during the crash, as well as a 'heavy' list to starboard. By that time, the inclination was only five degrees, but it would have been definitely noticeable by the passengers. Some friends – maybe Jones and Gee among them – found Barkworth there and they all climbed up to the Boat Deck, probably trying to find additional information about the accident.[10]

There, the group encountered Captain Edward John Smith himself. Ever the 'millionaire's captain',[11] he was surrounded by a crowd of crying women who

---

10. Account dictated to *Carpathia* passenger Mr Cecil R. Francis; *The New York Times*, 19 April 1912.

11. That was Smith's nickname due to his popularity among wealthy passengers.

wanted to know if the situation was serious. 'Go back to your cabins, ladies, and put on your lifebelts, and come back to the Boat Deck. I assure you there is no danger', the captain said. His deceivingly soothing speech did not fool Algy. 'I thought that sounded rather bad myself', he recalled, adding in another account that most of the passengers, on the other hand, were confident in the stability of the *Titanic*.[12]

Still in his evening attire, Barkworth complied with the captain's orders. He went down to his cabin one deck below and changed into warmer clothes: a heavy suit and then a fur coat. He finished up by strapping his life preserver on top of the coat. Extra cautious, Algy also packed a dispatch case (a kind of briefcase) with all of his money and some important papers before going back to the Boat Deck. When he passed the First Class Entrance to get outside, he was particularly moved by a tune being played by the ship's orchestra. 'I shall never forget the fierce jarring notes of that waltz they played', he remembered. Contrary to what cinematic versions of the sinking portrayed, the band was then playing inside the First Class Entrance instead of the open Boat Deck.[13]

About an hour had passed since the collision, and the evacuation process had already started. Women and children were being put into the lifeboats while the escaping steam from the ship's boilers made a deafening sound. The sight of panicked women leaving the

_____

12. *Hull Daily Mail*, 17 May 1912; *The New York Times*, 19 April 1912.

13. *Evening Banner*, 26 April 1912; Behe, George, 'Those Brave Fellows' – The Last Hours of the Titanic's Band, page 44.

Titanic deeply upset Barkworth. '...the officer began to man the lifeboats and fear seized upon the women, and the scenes were pathetic and awful in the extreme. I hate to think of them', he related to a reporter.[14]

The Englishman was able to reunite with his friends Gee and Jones but, unfortunately, his post-crash watchfulness had given way to a lack of concern. 'To tell the truth, I didn't think about getting into a lifeboat, and the boats were all gone before we realized the condition of the ship was so serious', he would reflect later to a reporter. In another interview, he chivalrously claimed to have stepped aside for women and children to board the boats, feeling 'it was no time to push forward'.[15]

Closer to the end, and perhaps now more conscious of the *Titanic's* fate, Algy returned to his cabin in order to retrieve more of his belongings only to find his door locked. This had been a precaution taken by stewards that night to prevent looting. He then returned to the Boat Deck again via the First Class Entrance and found it empty. The band's musicians had deserted their instruments for the time being; it is possible they were trying to find life jackets for themselves.

But a more likely explanation is that they realized they would have to go outside eventually and face the night's cold air and so had gone down to their rooms in order to retrieve some warmer clothes. Several passengers would claim to hear them just before the ship's final plunge, so Barkworth's sighting did not imply music on the *Titanic* had ceased to be played

14. *The New York Times*, 19 April 1912.

15. *Evening Banner*, 26 April 1912; *The New York Times*, 19 April 1912.

forever – he even suggested in an interview the musicians might have returned to their instruments after he had exited the First Class Entrance. Researcher George Behe, the foremost authority on the *Titanic's* band, concluded after examining the existing evidence that the orchestra started performing outside the Entrance at around 2 am – 20 minutes before the ship foundered.[16]

On the Boat Deck, Algy again found his friends Jones and Gee. But their reunion would be short-lived; the *Titanic* had little time left. The JP noticed that the liner began to list forward, and the trio decided to go aft. 'I remember somebody shouted: "Go gently!" as if a sudden shift of weight would have disturbed the ship's position!', he said later.

After that, the *Titanic's* bow gave what Barkworth called a 'premonitory dip' toward the ocean's depths – which he had read somewhere was a sign that a ship was about to sink. It presumably was the same movement described by Second Officer Charles Lightoller: 'a slight but definite plunge'. Now, the vessel was sinking at a much faster pace and her stern was rising higher into the air.

Their predicament was dire but, at that moment, Algy saw nobody around him particularly panicked or frightened. 'After all the boats had gone, everybody seemed to be waiting for death on the doomed ship', he remembered. Howard Case seemed more confident. Barkworth saw him on the Boat Deck and addressed the *Titanic's* imminent demise. 'My dear fel-

---

16. *Hull Daily Mail*, 17 May 1912; Behe, George, *'Those Brave Fellows' – The Last Hours of the Titanic's Band*, page 46.

low. I wouldn't think of quitting the ship. Why, she'll swim for a week', he answered, just before he calmly lit a cigarette.

It was clear to Algy that Case was awfully wrong. The Englishman had had enough of the *Titanic* and decided to leave her. At this moment, he saw the last of his two friends. 'Jones and Gee were standing by, with arms on the rail, looking down. I imagine they were preparing for death', he recalled. Barkworth bid them farewell by shaking their hands. Jones and Gee's bodies would eventually be recovered by the cable ship *Mackay-Bennett* and subsequently buried on land by their families and friends. Case's body, however, was never found.

It was time to abandon ship. Algy chucked his dispatch case into the vessel's waterways,[17] close to the edge of the Boat Deck. Then, he climbed up on the starboard bulwark and held onto a davit with one hand. The distance to the water below was only about 30 feet, about half of what it would normally be. The JP again noticed a big list and thought the *Titanic* was going to 'turn turtle'. Indeed, the vessel presented an approximate 10º list to port in her final moments.

'I hesitated for a few moments before dropping, for the sea seemed to be full of chairs and other wreckage thrown overboard by the passengers, and I

---

17. In one of his accounts, Algy said he had left his case in the scuppers, responsible for draining accumulated water into the sea. However, that is an impossibility, since there were no scuppers on the Boat Deck. The closest things that existed on the *Titanic*'s top level were the waterways, which led water to the scuppers. Given the similarity between the two mechanisms, it is more than likely that Barkworth simply mixed them up.

thought I should hurt myself. Fancy thinking of such a thing at such a time', he confided later.

Nevertheless, Algy stepped off.[18]

Point of no Return

Tatiana Yamshanova's painting that illustrates the cover of this book portrays Algernon holding onto Boat 7's then empty davits moments before he jumped off the ship. He never specified from where exactly he left the Titanic, but a careful analysis of Barkworth's accounts do point out that he was at the vicinity of Boat 7's davits at the end.

It is known Barkworth was on the starboard side because, according to his interview for the Hull Daily Mail, he was opposite the location where the band was playing when he departed the liner for good. The musicians began their performance inside the First Class Entrance, by the piano, which was on the port side. After he walked over to the starboard side, he mentioned his friends Arthur Gee and Charles Jones were there with their hands on the 'rail' (actually called bulwark), looking down. Fellow First Class passenger Howard Case was nearby, and Algernon talked briefly to him. The Justice of the Peace described that he then climbed up the bulwark and held onto a davit with one hand.

---

18. Account dictated to *Carpathia* passenger Mr Cecil R. Francis; *Evening Banner*, 26 April 1912; *Hull Daily Mail*, 17 May 1912; Lightoller, Charles, *Titanic and Other Ships*, page 127.

It is very likely he hung onto Boat 7's aft davit, because it fits his description perfectly. First of all, it is exactly opposite the First Class Entrance. Secondly, right next to the aft davit, there is a bulwark on which he could have stood and where Gee and Jones likely were leaning against. It would be a perfect spot to run into Case, because it was a part of the Boat Deck exclusive to First Class passengers. Finally, Lifeboat 7 was the most-aft boat in that First Class area, and Algernon said he and his friends went aft following the ship's 'first dip' – a probable mention of the moment when the Titanic's bow started going under. Why Barkworth would climb the bulwark is a mystery, because that would make his fall into the water higher and, thus, more dangerous. But that is exactly what he did. And, from all of the evidence presented above, he did it from the bulwark next to Boat 7's aft davit.

CHAPTER 2

Crossing the Humber

It was because of Algernon's privileged education at Eton College, which had included training in swimming, that he found the courage and skill to try his luck in the water.

His enrolment at Eton was sure indication of his family's social prominence. By the time he was born on 4 June 1864, the Barkworths had become one of the most wealthy and influential merchant families in East Yorkshire.

The Barkworths are a very old family, originating from a Lincolnshire village anciently known as Barkworth (Barcwurd). It has since divided in two, and they are now called East and West Barkwith, 30 miles away from Hessle. Historian John Elverson's research[19] revealed records of a Barkworth individual dating from the 12th century, and the surname starts appearing more frequently in 13th to 15th centuries' documents.

The first established records of Algernon's direct ancestors are from 1724, showing the Barkworths living in Nettleton, still in Lincolnshire. The *Titanic* survivor's great-grandfather, however, was to be

---

19. Elverson, John, *The Barkworth Family*, page 1 (unpublished).

born in Clee Old (now part of Cleethorpes), almost 14 miles away from Nettleton, in 1758. His name was John Barkworth.

Sometime after John's birth, his parents, Simon and Ann, decided to move to nearby Barton-upon-Humber with their four children. Being a merchant family, Simon and his youngest son John established a cabinet making business in the city, located at the south bank of the Humber River. When Simon died in 1782, John carried on with the family trade. The year before, the young man had married Elizabeth Potton, with whom he would have at least ten children.

John and Elizabeth decided to cross the Humber around 1792 and live in Sculcoates, which by that time was the industrial east end of the town of Kingston upon Hull (commonly referred to as just Hull)[20]. It was a decision that would change the future of the family forever.

Now on the northern bank of the river, John devoted himself to mahogany importing. He had already been importing timber from the Baltic before his move, but it was in Hull that his business would expand. Most of John's product came from Honduras, but he was also acquiring a better-quality mahogany called Spanish wood from Hispaniola Island and Cuba. He turned out so successful in this field that people started calling him Mahogany Jack. The former cabinet maker had become a rich merchant.

---

20. Hull only attained city status in 1897.

Mahogany Jack and his wife, Elizabeth,
were Algernon's great-grandparents
(Tony Edwards Collection[21])

Mahogany Jack had several partners in his timber merchant business, but the firm was better known as Barkworth & Spaldin. The timber yard was based on Hull's North Dockside.

The Barkworths decided to move out of Hull in order to get away from the overcrowding and dirtiness of the town now that they had the means to do it. Hessle proved to be an ideal location because it was less than five miles away from Hull and thus close enough to commute to work. They were not alone in their decision, as Hessle and other nearby villages started

21. Paintings kindly provided by John Elverson.

becoming the home for a number of other rich merchants, ship owners and bankers.[22]

In 1805, Jack bought an extensive piece of land of about 17 acres and had a mansion built on its grounds by the next year. It was named Tranby House, given that the plot used to be a part of Tranby Field, and it became a symbol of his fortune and influence. Tranby House continued to serve as the home for the Barkworth family for the next 140 years and is still in existence today.

The mansion consists of two main storeys, with attics and a basement; five bays, with the three central ones projecting slightly forward under a pediment; a Doric porch and a hipped roof. It was built of cream brick with white stone dressings. As expected, much of the woodwork and furniture was made of mahogany,

---

22. *Tranby House* - https://sites.google.com/site/tranbyhouse/home, visited on 25 December 2021.

including the doors and the staircase, which featured marble treads.

According to research conducted by historian Michael Free, the main block of the house had a drawing room, library, morning room, dining room, kitchen, servants' hall, butler's pantry, boxroom, cloak room and other smaller rooms on the ground floor. The drawing room was covered in green and gold wallpaper and paintings decorated the dining room's walls.

On the first floor, there were seven bedrooms, three dressing rooms and a water closet (a compartment with a toilet in it). A brew house, wash house and stable block could be found at the rear of the mansion, with drying and ironing rooms and four other storerooms on top of them. There was also a separate garage block.

The servants slept in the attics above the first floor and men and women had separate rooms, reached by different staircases. 'The driveway to the house featured a long, sweeping avenue filled on either side with a wide range of plants, which provided a pleasant approach at all times of the year', added Free. All in all, the mansion boasted 25 rooms.

Free also found out that Mahogany Jack was involved in a research project with the Admiralty, whose goal was finding high-quality wood to be used in its ships. So, Barkworth did some experiments. He discovered that better-quality timber could be obtained by stripping the bark from mature oaks and leaving the trunks in the ground for three years.

Tranby House in the 1900s
(Justin Lowe Collection)

One of Tranby House's driveways (Justin Lowe Collection)

Despite all the wealth earned from his timber importing business, Mahogany Jack would soon branch out into other fields. With his partner, George Hawkes, he established a shipbuilding yard at Hessle Cliff, on the banks of the Humber River, around 1811 – his new enterprise uncreatively named Barkworth & Hawkes. The yard operated until 1835 and was responsible for building warships for the Royal Navy and trading vessels, especially East Indiamen. The Indiamen were large ships used for trade between Europe and South Asia and represented a significant addition to the family's increasing interests in the far east. With this in mind, it is easy to see why Jack also started investing in shipping, trading mainly with the East Indies. However, this venture would only truly blossom through his descendants.

Two of the more famous ships built by Barkworth & Hawkes were Navy bomb vessels named the *Hecla* and the *Infernal*. They were launched in 1815 and participated in the bombardment of Algiers, Algeria, a

successful effort by Britain and The Netherlands to end the local practices of piracy and slavery. The heavily built *Hecla* made her strong enough to withstand the obstacles presented by artic weather, and thus she was used for exploring the northern seas in several voyages from 1819 to 1827.[23]

The Barkworths were instrumental in developing the small, rural Hessle community. In 1806, when the family settled there, the population did not exceed 700. Most locals were farmers or worked in chalk quarries, but Hessle boasted a small commercial area with shops and professional men such as doctors and solicitors. The arrival of Mahogany Jack and his timber, shipyard and shipping businesses catalysed their economic evolution, providing more job opportunities. In 1901, the population of Hessle was 3,918. The village grew almost six-fold in the 19th century; by comparison, England's inhabitants fell a little short of quadrupling in the same period.

---

23. Free, M. G., *The House of Barkworth*, pages 1-2 and 12-13, Hessle Local Historical Society, 2016 (unpublished); *The September Meeting: Tranby House and the Barkworths*, pages 11-12, Hessle Local History Society – Newsletter no. 83, courtesy of East Riding Archives; *The Barkworth family and Tranby House, Hessle*, page 10, Hessle Local History Society – Newsletter no. 75, courtesy of M. G. Free; Elverson, John, *The Barkworth Family*, pages 4-5 and 9 (unpublished); *Tranby House* - https://sites.google.com/site/tranbyhouse/, visited on 03 April 2022.

The Shipyard at Hessle Cliff (1820), by John Wilson Carmichael. The business was owned by Mahogany Jack and his partner, George Hawkes (Wikimedia Commons)

More than becoming part of the local elite, the Barkworths cared for the community's wellbeing. Charity work had always been a key characteristic of the family. When Mahogany Jack died in 1815, newspapers described him as a 'husband and father of the most tender affection and a liberal benefactor to the poor'. It is worth noting that he was against slavery. After Jack's death, Elizabeth continued living at Tranby House until 1838, when she, too, passed away. Their eldest son, also named John, inherited the mansion, where he started living with his family.

The younger John Barkworth married Emma Boulderson in 1818, when he was about 30 years old, and the couple went on to have 15 children, including Algernon's father, Henry. There is evidence that Tranby House was extended at some point; this may have happened around 1839, when there was a real need to more comfortably accommodate Barkworth's large family.[24]

An able entrepreneur like his father, John expanded the family's businesses. One of his actions was to set up yet another firm, Barkworth & Co., which dealt exclusively with shipping.

The Barkworth fleet grew under John's keen leadership. In 1806, they had only one ship of 267 tons trading with the West Indies, but there were 18 of them by 1815, including vessels sailing the Baltic waters. Four years later, Barkworth & Co. even had two whalers

24. *Tranby House* - https://sites.google.com/site/tranbyhouse/, visited on 25 December 2021; Free, M. G., *The House of Barkworth*, pages 4-5, Hessle Local History Society, 2016 (unpublished); *The September Meeting: Tranby House and the Barkworths*, page 11, Hessle Local History Society – Newsletter no. 83, courtesy of East Riding Archives.

*John Barkworth, the younger, and his wife, Emma
(Left – Christopher Elverson Collection /
Right - John Elverson Collection)*

hunting whales and seals in the South Seas.[25] Some vessels went as far as Central and South America as well as the East Indies. Among the company's ships, there were the Barkworth, the Potton, the Dowson and the Elizabeth. The family was thought to have owned over 20 ships altogether.

As for Barkworth & Spaldin, the firm opened branches in Grimsby, Gloucester and London, where its offices were located in Pall Mall.[26] Out of all the family businesses, John was mainly a timber merchant, as

25. Elverson, John, *The Barkworth Family*, page 9 (unpublished).

26. *Tranby House* - https://sites.google.com/site/tranbyhouse/, visited on 25 December 2021; *The September Meeting: Tranby House and the Barkworths*, pages 10-11, Hessle Local History Society – Newsletter no. 83, courtesy of East Riding Archives.

two of his sons would also later become – including Algernon's father.

Just like Mahogany Jack, his son John donated large amounts of money to the poor and was interested in giving them a better life. Maybe it was the desire for social equality that led him into politics. He was elected Alderman to the Corporation of Hull (the town's then governing body) in the 1820s. John Elverson explains well what an Alderman did:

> 'From 1331 to 1835 Hull was governed by 13 Aldermen, collectively known as the Bench, one of whom was elected as Mayor. The position of Alderman was for life. The Aldermen ran the town making all the decisions about its services and governance. The Mayor was the head of the corporation and the Chief Magistrate. It was his duty to sit every day, Sundays excepted, at the Guildhall to hear complaints, and to dispose of the general magisterial business'.[27]

It was a tradition for the Aldermen to take turns in becoming Mayor of Kingston upon Hull. In September of 1832, by a vote of 688 to 83, John Barkworth was elected to the town's highest post for a yearly term. He would later declare that it was his turn to take up the position, which was unremunerated. Besides being Mayor and Chief Magistrate, Barkworth held the

---

27. Elverson, John, *The Barkworth Family*, page 9 (unpublished).

honorary title of Admiral of the Humber.[28] Coincidentally, his grandson Algernon would years later become a Hull magistrate himself and judge the cases of the region's inhabitants.

'He [John Barkworth] seems to have carried out these roles with diligence and ability and to have gained the respect of those he served', wrote Michael Free. 'Holding the office of Mayor or Sheriff was both prestigious and expensive. The holders were expected to meet many expenses out of their own pockets. They were, for example, expected to meet delegations and entertain other dignitaries at their own expense.... John Barkworth was a highly capable and much-respected figure in nineteenth-century Hull'.[29]

During his tenure as Mayor, John erected a memorial to the recently deceased William Wilberforce, a leader of the anti-slavery movement. A native of Hull, Wilberforce had risen high to become a Member of Parliament for Yorkshire. Mahogany Jack had been one of his supporters.

John died on 28 March 1846 after a long illness. Emma stayed at Tranby House for some time, but she eventually moved out. The widow apparently spent a lot of her time living with relatives in other parts of the country. Emma might have returned to live in the mansion around 1872, her presence there being recorded in Kelly's Directory of that year. She died four years

---

28. Raymond, John, *Descendants of Emma Boulderson* – http://freepages.rootsweb.com/~jray/genealogy/boulderson/emma.htm, visited on 25 December 2021.

29. Free, M. G., *The House of Barkworth*, pages 5-6, Hessle Local History Society, 2016 (unpublished).

later and was buried in the family vault at the village of Kirk Ella, on the outskirts of Hull.

Under normal circumstances, the oldest son would become the new owner of an estate after the death of his parents. But, in an interesting turn of events, Tranby House was inherited by John and Emma's third son, Henry, born in 1822.

That came to be because Henry's two older brothers, John Boulderson and Shadwell, had plans of their own. John was the oldest and, like his father, focused on the timber branch of the family's businesses. He lived in Hull but moved to London when the firm opened an office there. He married, had two daughters and the family lived in different places throughout the years. They finally settled in 1890 after acquiring an estate in the town of Havant, in Hampshire County, almost 200 miles away from Hessle. Shadwell, the next in line, took Holy Orders, something common for second sons of upper-class families of the time. He was ordained a deacon and went on to occupy several posts in the south of England.

After their parents' deaths, Henry continued to live at Tranby House. According to John Elverson's research, John Boulderson made a deal with his brother over the property, presumably because he no longer lived in Hull at the time. Henry could inherit the mansion if he gave his older brother half of an estate he owned in Lincolnshire. The exchange was carried out, and Henry officially became the new owner of Tranby House.

Henry married Catherine Smith in 1858. One of their children, George Henry, died in infancy, but the other four reached adulthood: Edmund (born in 1859), Evelyn (1860), Algernon (1864) and Violet (1866). Like his

Algernon's parents, Catherine and Henry Barkworth
(Justin Lowe Collection)

older brother, father and grandfather, Henry became a timber merchant, managing Barkworth & Spaldin until it was sold to Thorpe, Balfour & Harrison in 1888.[30]

Algernon's father expanded the family's already varied economic fields and, starting in 1871, declared in census forms that he was a farmer. The Barkworths had land in Hessle and the Easenby farm in the nearby village of Swanland, part of which is still farmed today – most of Easenby is now a housing state.[31] By 1881, Henry had 60 acres of land of his own.

30. *Tranby House* - https://sites.google.com/site/tranbyhouse/, visited on 26 February 2022; Free, M. G., *The House of Barkworth*, pages 6-8, Hessle Local History Society, 2016 (unpublished); Elverson, John, *The Barkworth Family*, pages 10 and 12 (unpublished); Raymond, John, *Descendants of Emma Boulderson* –

http://freepages.rootsweb.com/~jray/genealogy/boulderson/emma.htm, visited on 25 December 2021.

31. *Tranby House* - https://sites.google.com/site/tranbyhouse/, visited on 1 January 2022; M. G. Free's personal correspondence with this author.

Evelyn (left) and Violet Barkworth
(Justin Lowe Collection)

CHAPTER 3

An undistinguished football player

After three generations, the Barkworth family had successfully cemented itself as part of the economic, social and political elite of Hessle and nearby Hull. Ever since his birth in 1864, Algy benefited from this advantageous position, enjoying a lifestyle which can best be described as posh.

Little is known about his first years, but they certainly were not harsh. Living at Tranby House, the boy's needs would be overseen by seven to nine servants[32] – butlers, coachmen, footmen, cooks, housemaids, dairymaids, kitchen maids, nurses and laundresses among them. There was also a governess named Amelia Coxhead, who raised Henry and Catherine's children and remained in the employ of the family for many years.

_____

32. According to census records, Tranby House had seven servants in 1861, eight in 1871 and nine in 1881. Available at *Tranby House* - https://sites.google.com/site/tranbyhouse/home, visited on 25 December 2021.

Algernon Wilson?

A few sources claim Algernon's complete name is Algernon Henry Wilson Barkworth. During this book's research process, hundreds of reports and documents on Algernon were analysed, including his baptism and death certificates, which stated Algernon Henry Barkworth. None of them disclosed 'Wilson' as his middle name. However, four reports from the Hull Daily Mail *could make a very flimsy case for those who defend that theory.*

The first source dates from 16 December 1892, and mentions that a certain 'Mr. A. Wilson Barkworth' was present at the Conservative Association for the Welton District's annual banquet. This could very well have been Algernon, since he identified himself as a conservative from a young age. But a likelier candidate is Arthur Bromby Wilson-Barkworth, a solicitor from Hull who became a member of the family by marriage.

The second and third incidents, dated July 1909 and August 1912, respectively, could also relate to Algy, since they report events organized by Conservatives in the Hull and Hessle area. They both mention the attendance of a certain 'A. W. Barkworth, J. P.' The last report is an advert from January 1942: 'A. W. Barkworth', from Tranby House, was hiring a house parlourmaid.

All four mentions could have been the result of a typo, a common trait of that era's press. And we do not even know if the person in the 1892 story was really Algernon – he most likely was not. So, it is safe to deduce his full name was Algernon Henry Barkworth.

When he was less than a month shy of his 14th birthday, on 8 May 1878, Algy was enrolled at Eton College, located in the city of the same name, almost 155 miles away from Hessle.

Being at boarding school, Barkworth started to live in one of Eton's several Houses. His House Master – the teacher who runs the students' quarters – was Reverend Charles Caldecott James, who would later become the rector in the village of Wortham in Suffolk County. As an Eton pupil, the boy would be educated in subjects such as French, Greek, Latin, mathematics, physics and history.[33] Based on his *Titanic* accounts, he also learned how to swim there.

Eton records strangely reveal that Barkworth only studied there until 1879. Why would he leave one of the best schools in the country at 15? The reason is unknown, but the school newspaper, *The Eton College Chronicle*, could provide a clue. Edited by the students, it mentions Algy only twice in his short stay at the school. Supervised by Reverend James, the boy, along with his football team, competed in an internal championship named Lower Boy Cup. They won a match on 14 November 1878, by 3 to 1, but their hope of winning the Cup was crushed on the 23rd, when they lost by 1

---

33. Information courtesy of Eton Archives.

*Algy at Eton, in 1878 or 1879: he is in the centre of the
right photo, with his brother Edmund behind him
(John Elverson Collection)*

to 0. In both instances, the *Chronicle* recorded the best
players of the matches, and Barkworth was not mentioned in either one.[34]

By comparison, his older brother, Edmund, also
studied at Eton, from 1873 to 1877, or from when he was
14 to 18 years old. His mentions in the school paper
were much more frequent, totalling 20 in all. Edmund,
too, was a mediocre football player, but also engaged
in other sports like rowing, at which he excelled. His
performance was occasionally complimented by the

---

34. *The Eton College Chronicle*, 28 November 1878, and 19 December 1878.

young reporters; he was once made captain of his boat, and in 1877 he rowed for Eton at the Henley Royal Regatta, one of the most famous and prestigious events of its kind in the world.

'Although we did not even win our Heat,[35] it cannot be said that our crew has in any way disgraced itself, but has, on the contrary, gained as much praise as those of former years', wrote the *Chronicle* about the team's performance in the competition.[36] After having graduated from Eton, Edmund returned to row at least twice in the school races. Coincidentally or not, Eton possesses two individual photos of Edmund in its archives, but none of Algy.

The younger Barkworth, however, appears in three group shots, depicting the House led by Reverend James. In the photos, taken in 1878 and 1879,[37] he does not look at the camera. Of course, in those days posing was a much longer, formal and uncomfortable activity, and many of the students look serious and are seen facing away from the camera, but Algy's face and body language give an impression of sadness and aloofness. Even though he was surrounded by tens of his schoolmates and his House Master, Barkworth seemed out of his element.

---

35. Races which determine which teams are disqualified and which ones advance in the competition.

36. *The Eton College Chronicle*, 7 July 1877.

37. Two of the group photos were taken in 1878, and probably on the same day, as they show the same individuals in the same positions and posing similarly. For the sake of simplicity, this book reproduces only one of the 1878 images.

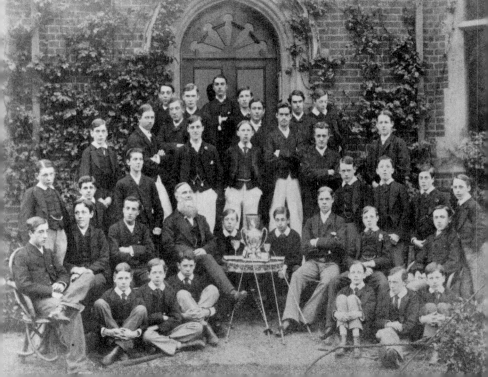

The available evidence could indicate that Algy was not a star pupil and might not have adapted to the school's routine and/or community. In his *Titanic* accounts, he mentions only being educated at Eton, but he probably enrolled in another school after 1879. In the 1881 census, when Barkworth was almost 17, he was absent from the Tranby House record, perhaps because he was away at another boarding school.

What the young man did after graduation is equally unclear. Different sources claim he studied Law at either Oxford or Cambridge Universities, but it is almost certain he did not pursue any higher education. Oxford Archives' staff declared that there are no records of him ever attending the university up to 1892.[38] As for Cambridge, Algy's name is nowhere to be found on any of the alumni listings through 1912, although other Barkworth family members do appear in the files, like his uncles Harold and Alfred.

It is probable that, after completing secondary school in the early 1880s, Algy simply started to enjoy the good life that his family's wealth and status allowed him to lead. He eventually returned to Tranby House and, like many of his relatives, became active in the region's social events.

---

38. Oxford Archives' personal correspondence with this author.

Group photos from Reverend James's House at Eton College from 1878 (top) and 1879. Algy is in the bottom row in the 1878 picture, the fifth from left to right. In the 1879 image, he can be seen sitting on a chair, again in the foreground, at the far left (Reproduced by permission of the Provost and Fellows of Eton College)

A young Algy Barkworth, ca. 1882
(John Elverson Collection)

Barkworth is first mentioned in the *Hull Daily Mail*, the region's main newspaper, in May 1886, age 21. He sent a letter of apology for not attending a meeting whose goal was to form a habitation (a local branch) of the Primrose League, an organisation known for spreading Conservative principles in Great Britain. The first known event at which he was present was an annual ball in connection with a fox hunting affair called the Holderness Hunt. The event took place in January 1887 in the town of Beverley, some 8 ½ miles from Hessle, and was also attended by his father and his aunt Dora, wife of John Boulderson[39].

He was his brother Edmund's best man when he married Clara Reid, known as 'Ada', in June 1890. Algy, his parents and sisters, relatives and friends travelled to the town of Cheltenham (143 miles away from Hessle) to participate in the ceremony, staying at the luxurious Queen's Hotel.

Barkworth would attend several family members, friends, and acquaintances' weddings in future years, including his sister Violet's to their cousin Harold Pease in July 1891. On these special occasions, Algy used to give refined gifts, like an inlaid table, a case of silver dessert knives and forks, a carved stool, a silver candlestick, a travelling clock in a case, a decanter, a Pyrex, a silver dish and even a silver muffineer (a fancy name for a saltshaker).[40]

---

39. *Hull Daily Mail*, 4 May 1886; *The Driffield Times and General Adviser*, 22 January 1887.

40. *Cheltenham Chronicle*, 21 June 1890; *Cheltenham Looker-On*, 21 June 1890; *Yorkshire Gazette*, 25 July 1891; *Hull Daily Mail*, 2 June 1934; Raymond, John, *Descendants of Emma Boulderson* – http://freepages.rootsweb.com/~jray/genealogy/boulderson/emma.htm, visited on 25 December 2021.

Algy (sitting, holding a hat) was the best man at his brother Edmund's wedding to Ada Reid in 1890 (Justin Lowe Collection)

In November 1896, he was present at the Hessle Conservative Association's anniversary dinner, proposing a toast to the press on the occasion, and joined the committee responsible for organising the commemoration of Queen Victoria's Diamond Jubilee at Hessle in June 1897.[41]

Like his grandfather, Barkworth was politically active and very involved with the social issues of his peers. He identified himself as a conservative, was chosen vice-president of his hometown's Conservative Club in 1896, and was re-elected for the same position the following year.[42] He was a unionist[43] and always participated in social gatherings of the political associations of which he was a member, such as anniversary dinners.[44]

A few days after the outbreak of the Second Boer War in November 1899, Algy donated five pounds and five shillings (approximately £604 today) for a fund to help widows and orphans of soldiers killed in action and disabled combatants. As for the donation fund for restoring the Holy Trinity Church (now Hull Minster) in 1901, he contributed five pounds, and five years later the same cause elicited a much more generous offer from him: 100 pounds, which today would correspond

---

41. *Hull Daily Mail*, 30 November 1896, and 23 June 1897.

42. *Hull Daily Mail*, 1 July 1896; *Eastern Morning News*, 13 August 1897.

43. *Yorkshire Post and Leeds Intelligencer*, 16 July 1909; *Hull Daily Mail*, 3 December 1909. Unionism is a political ideology favouring the continued unity of England, Scotland, Wales and Northern Ireland as one sovereign state.

44. *York Herald*, 21 January 1893.

to the huge sum of £11,000. Barkworth was also a member of the Hull Discharged Prisoners' Aid Society.[45]

The young man was no stranger to more physical activities, being a frequent participant of the Holderness Hunts. He often had the company of his younger sister, Violet. In 1891 and 1895, Algy held the position of vice-president in the organising committee of the Working Men's Sports, a race competition comprised of several categories. The events attracted a large number of spectators, and its proceeds were donated to the local Sick Fund.[46]

Barkworth also acted as a judge for a sporting tournament in 1896 at the house of his friend and neighbour H. R. Maxstead, which displayed curious contests such as 'potato-picking for girls', 'egg and spoon race for boys' and a 'three-legged race for married men'. Three years later, Algy was elected one of the vice-presidents of the Hessle Cricket Club. Although Barkworth eventually developed interests for more sedentary pastimes, he at least maintained the outside impression that he was still an athlete of sorts in his later years – newspapers reporting his presence on the *Titanic* described him as a 'typical British sportsman'. By then, Algy was 47.[47]

It would be with Maxstead that Barkworth ventured away for the first time from the family business-

45. *Eastern Morning News*, 7 November 1899; *Hull Daily Mail*, 23 January 1901, 2 November 1906, and 10 August 1909.

46. *Hull Daily Mail*, 19 May 1891, and 4 June 1895; *East Riding Telegraph*, 8 June 1895.

47. *East Riding Telegraph*, 15 August 1896; *Eastern Morning News*, 1 December 1899; *The Yorkshire Post*, 27 April 1912.

es and tried to make a name for himself. The company with which he intended to achieve that goal was The Anglesey Trading Company.

The firm was set up in 1896 in the village of Llanfechell on the Welsh island of Anglesey by Barkworth, Maxstead and the local Colonel Owen Thomas. Algy and H. R. were holidaying in Llanfechell when they were approached by Thomas. He persuaded them to become partners in his firm, which was then renamed the Anglesey Trading Company. It employed about 80 men of all trades at its peak (including weavers, cartmen, tinmen, blacksmiths, saddlers, cobblers, painters, valuers, coopers, clerks and labourers) and was said to be able to take up any job in the area.

Anglesey traded in all kinds of goods, sold building supplies, dealt in houses and other properties, and carried on the enterprises of builders, contractors and manufacturers. The company's business consisted mainly of a shop that sold ironmongery, saddlery and earthenware. Despite all these lines of work, Anglesey was never successful; the firm signed several contracts to build schools, houses, a chapel and even a hotel, but every single one of them failed to make a profit. Algy would retire from the company in 1898, selling his shares to Colonel Thomas. The enterprise ended up closing its doors in 1899, after only three years of existence.[48]

A British gentleman named Richard Jones visited Llanfechell sometime after the Second World War and wrote an account of Anglesey's short lifespan. In it,

---

48. Free, M. G., *Algernon Henry Barkworth*, pages 1-2, Hull History Centre Records (unpublished); *The North Wales Chronicle*, 15 September 1900.

Barkworth is portrayed as unprepared to helm such a venture and out of touch with the local labourers:

> 'Neither Maxted [sic] or Barkworth had any experience of running such a business. Both of them were suspicious of the workers because they did not understand their language. They employed two English clerks from Rhyl [a Welsh town] to look after 'things'! The workers took offence at this attitude, and it was thought that some of them yielded to dishonesty, because the doubts were there already. Others thought that Maxted and Barkworth were much too ambitious, and therefore in too much of a hurry to expand. They bought too much at a time, for example they would [buy] many loads of coffin decorations and tens of thousands of shoelaces! The demand was never equal to the order (fortunately when one thinks of the thousands of coffin plates!). It's no wonder that the shoelaces were still in circulation in 1943! Maxted was a very generous man, but Barkworth on the other hand was a real miser. The latter lost a penny on the storehouse floor once and spent a whole morning looking for it!*
>
> The Gadlys Hotel in Cemaes [a village on Anglesey] was built by the company without estimating the cost. When

Owen Thomas made an application for a licence for the Gadlys, he was turned down by the magistrates at Amlwch because of the strong spirit of temperance in the land. The fine hotel had to be sold cheaply as a private residence to a Colonel Wilson. Gadlys is only one example of the heavy losses that the ATC made.[49]

Jones might have been too severe when analysing Algy. It is possible Barkworth was just frugal instead of a miser. Frugality was a trait that many upper-class English people of that time shared. Even the titled class and royalty were known to pinch pennies; financial extravagance and showiness was more American than British.[50]

1898 started out tragically for Algy and his family. On 13 January, his father, Henry, died, just two days before his 76th birthday. The funeral took place four days later at the village of Kirk Ella and was attended by a large gathering of friends and family members, Algy included. 'Mr. Barkworth was formerly a timber merchant in Hull, being of the firm of Messrs Barkworth and Spaldin. Since retiring from that business, he devoted his time to farming at Hessle. He was very be-

49. *Anglesey Trading Company 1896 - 1899*. Link: http://www.cymdeithashanesmechell.co.uk/atcs.html, visited on 3 November 2021.

50. Randy Bryan Bigham's personal correspondence with this author.

Henry Barkworth
(Justin Lowe Collection)

nevolent, giving liberally to the poor of the village, and until recently contributed £50 per year to the Curates' Fund', said the *Hull Daily Mail*, which observed several of Henry's farm servants were among the bearers of his coffin. Maybe it was a gesture of gratitude, since the Barkworths were known for being good landlords (*see* *'The mystery of Stanley House' on page 125*).

Henry's estate was valued at £151,365 (equal to £17,200,000 currently) and his net personal assets, £130,072. Barkworth left Tranby House and an allowance of £1,800 per year for his wife, Catherine. Algy was willed the Easenby farm at Swanland and other lands in the nearby village of West Ella, and the residue of his father's real and personal estates was divided into equal shares with his brother Edmund. Henry's daughters Evelyn and Violet received £7,500 and £2,500 in stocks, respectively. Even Amelia Coxhead, who had raised Henry's children, was remembered with an annuity of £60.[51]

Algy, it seems, took an instant liking to Easenby. In September 1898, only six months after inheriting it, he revived an old custom and threw a Harvest Home supper in the farm's barn, which was 'tastefully decorated' for the occasion. The Harvest Home, also called Ingathering, is a traditional English festival. Its participants celebrate the last day of harvest by singing, shouting and decorating their villages with boughs.

---

51. *Hull Daily Mail*, 17 January 1898; *Illustrated London News*, 23 April 1898.

Easenby Farm today (Hessle Local History Society Archive)

Around this time, Barkworth also started attending events in the village, such as the laying of a mission chapel's foundation stone in July 1899. He even handed out the prizes for collections of fruit, flowers and vegetables in the 1902 Swanland Flower Show.[52]

Under Algy's supervision, Easenby flourished and, at least until the mid-1920s, the Englishman was considered one of the three main landowners on Swanland.[53]

Education at Swanland must have been a topic of great interest to Barkworth because he became one of the managers of the village's school in 1898. Managers were responsible for the finances of the school and the

52. *Hull Daily Mail*, 17 July 1899, and 4 August 1902.

53. *Hull Daily Mail*, 23 September 1898; *Yorkshire, North & East Ridings, Kelly's Directory*, 1925.

Algy is seen sitting behind a dog on her sister Violet's marriage to Harold Pease in 1891 (Justin Lowe Collection)

building's maintenance and could also appoint pupil and student teachers to reinforce the school's staff.

In 1903, the managers decided the institution should become a voluntary non-provided school. That meant that the upkeep of the building would still be the manager's responsibility, but the newly formed East Riding Local Education Authority (LEA) would begin to fund the payment of teachers and teaching materials. Algy was then elected as one of the school's four Foundation Governors. He was surely involved in alterations to the school building in 1904, which included paving the playground, the repair of the pond wall, building a new cloakroom and the inclusion of additional ventilation.[54]

It is not known if Barkworth was given the Swanland farm because he was fond of animals or if it was this new possession that sparked his interest in them. It is possible he always liked them; at age 27, he was pictured sitting behind a dog on the occasion of his sister Violet's wedding in 1891. Two years later, Algy was present at a 'puppy judging' of the dogs and bitches that would participate in the Holderness Hunts, an animal-centred activity he attended ever since he was a young man.

However, the fact remains that Barkworth started surrounding himself with animals more and more throughout the years. He appeared to have assumed a more active role in the management of his farm in 1907 (up until then, it is likely his bailiffs ran the farm for

54. Dalby, Shirley, Brooks, Derek, Holmes, John, *A New History of Swanland – The School and the Twentieth Century*, pages 14, 18, 20 and 22. Courtesy or Justin Lowe.

him), as the newspapers began to report his buying and selling of sheep and cattle and, occasionally, horses.

Two years later, Algy won two awards in a horse show in the agricultural mare or gelding categories. His prized animal in one of the classes was a brown gelding named Banker, described by the press as 'only three years old, long and low, though firmly coupled, and very compact'. In 1910, Barkworth would win first place in another competition, this time in the hackney gelding or filly class. Agriculture was an interest of his, too, and the newspapers recorded him attending meetings of the Holderness Agricultural Club.[55]

Barkworth had a passion for all things mechanical as well and, in the 1890s, a novelty grabbed his attention: the motor car. He started buying automobiles and motorcycles, including a Rolls Royce and a large roadster which he named 'Dixie'. He was one of the first citizens of the Hull area to acquire cars and probably one of the first in England.[56] The Honourable Evelyn Henry Ellis was the first to import an automobile, a Panhard et Levassor, into the UK in June 1895. By 1900, when national production of cars had already begun, there were 700 to 800 automobiles circling on Britain's roads.

----

55. *Yorkshire Gazette*, 12 August 1893; *Driffield Times*, 21 September 1907; *Hull Daily Mail*, 17 December 1907, 13 April 1909, 17 April 1909, 11 December 1909, 4 May 1910, 9 July 1910, and 31 January 1917; *Crewe Chronicle*, 24 August 1912.

56. *Hull Daily Mail*, 06 April 1927, and 27 April 1928; Edwards, Brian, *A Swim for Dear Life – The True Story of a Titanic Survivor*, page 5. Courtesy of Bruce Robinson; Free, M. G., *Algernon Henry Barkworth*, page 2, Hull History Centre Records (unpublished).

Algy (right) and his brother Edmund (left) posing on a farm, possibly Easenby (John Elverson Collection)

Given it was an emerging industry, Algy faced a few hiccups when he was just starting his collection. One of them even made its way to the courts. In May 1900, his case was heard before a judge and jury.

He had ordered an Orient Express car in 1898 from the London-based Automobile Association, for which he had already paid £75 out of its cost of £201. But Barkworth was not satisfied with the machine and reached an agreement with the company; he would accept a Barriere tricycle instead, which sold for 75 guineas. When the tricycle was delivered, the Englishman was disappointed to find out it was not correctly painted. To make matters worse, the three-wheeled vehicle did not work properly and had to be shipped back for repairs.

The company agreed to send him a new one, but Algy would have none of it when he found out at an event that it was an old model. 'I did not wish the people in London to think me a flat', he justified in court regarding his refusal, just before he produced a show card, presumably written by the Automobile Association, announcing the tricycle had been built especially for Algernon Henry Barkworth. He managed to win the case and received £89 plus costs.[57]

With the fast expansion of the automobile industry, Hull began to adapt itself to the needs of drivers, and in 1906 a garage was opened in the city. Algy was of course present at the unveiling event and must have appreciated the new premises. He now had a place not only to refuel his cars but also a site that provided services like the selling of tires and accessories, repairs, parking for lengthy periods of time and washing. And, to cap it all, the garage was open 24 hours a day.

Algy even took his cars on trips abroad, as he was reported to have taken his Sunbeam automobile for a French tour in 1923. 'Mr Barkworth described the experience as interesting, but he said he preferred Devonshire scenery', the *Hull Daily Mail* wrote.[58]

---

57. Edwards, Brian, *A Swim for Dear Life – The True Story of a Titanic Survivor*, page 5. Courtesy of Bruce Robinson; *Hull Daily Mail*, 29 May 1900.

58. *Hull Daily Mail*, 13 July 1906, and 14 June 1923.

In the left photo, Algernon (left) and his brother Edmund ride in an early motor car at Tranby House; Algy is seen in the same car in the right photo. Perhaps both were taken on the same day, as he is wearing a white hat and with a wooden lap robe, both of which are seen in the left photo (Justin Lowe Collection)

*Algy at the wheel of one of his cars
(Justin Lowe Collection)*

Two more photos of Algy in one of his automobiles. Perhaps there are so many photos of Barkworth in cars because he was also a photography enthusiast (Justin Lowe Collection)

Photography was another interest of his; maybe that is why there are so many pictures of Barkworth in motor cars, as can be seen on the previous pages. He converted one of Tranby House's rooms into a studio and dark room. Michael Free thinks that the photograph reproduced at the beginning of Chapter 1 shows the magistrate sitting in this room before the refurbishments. The background in the image is a set, which he possibly had specially made. Free also revealed that Algy involved some of his servants in this activity by getting them to pose. At least one of them was trained by Barkworth in the photography craft.[59]

However, researcher Justin Lowe has another theory on the location where the famous portrait was taken, and it is more substantiated than Free's assessment. Lowe is the owner of the original photograph of Algy and on its back there is the address of a photo studio called The Franco British Art Co., with branches in Dublin, Ireland, and Manchester. There is no record of Barkworth ever visiting either city, but he could very well have posed for a portrait during a vacation trip since he liked travelling so much. The Manchester studio is the likeliest one to have taken the photo, the city being only around 75 miles from Hessle.

There is another argument that points towards the image being snapped in a studio rather than at Tranby House: there is at least one more photograph taken by The Franco British Art Co. whose background

59. *Hessle Photos and History* Facebook Group, 18 April 2021; Free, M. G., *Algernon Henry Barkworth*, page 3, Hull History Centre Records (unpublished); M. G. Free's personal correspondence with this author.

set is the very same one used on Barkworth's portrait (see on the next page). So, it seems quite likely that the famous Algy photo shows him during a holiday either in Manchester or Ireland[60].

At the turn of the century, the Englishman was approaching 40 years of age, and perhaps by that time he thought his idyllic life lacked meaning. That could be the reason for his moving to the Piddletrenthide village and becoming the next-door neighbour of his brother Edmund and his family. He appears living there in March 1901, when the national census was carried out. Dorothy, the four-year-old daughter of Edmund and Ada, would grow up to become a favourite of Algy's. This close relationship might have begun in that little village in Dorset County.[61]

––––––––––––

60. 60 . During this book's proofreading stage, M. G. Free challenged Justin Lowe's theory. 'It is...possible that the company came to Hessle to take photos of Barkworth.... Wealthy families tended to have photographers come to them rather than go to the photographers', he explained in a personal message to this author. According to Free, most photographers of that era would have taken their backdrops around with them - some still do. The back of the photos would have been stamped by these professionals with the name of their studios.

61. M. G. Free, in personal correspondence with this author, expressed his opinion that Algy was only visiting Piddletrenthide at this time. Barkworth would go on a spring holiday annually, an occasion which prompted Tranby House to be shut down for a month or so. He believes his choice destination in 1901 was the village where his brother lived. However, at that same time, Catherine and Evelyn were still at Tranby House and it seems odd that Algy would travel to see Edmund without his immediate family. Besides, if he really was a visitor, he could have been recorded as such in the census forms.

From left to right: Algy, Catherine, Henry (Edmund's son), Evelyn, Dorothy and Edmund at Tranby House (John Elverson Collection)

John Barton (standing) and Pat Barton's portrait taken by The Franco British Art Co. studio; notice the background set is the same on Algy's photo pictured at the beginning of Chapter 1 (Michael Kilcommons Collection / Randy Bryan Bigham)

But Barkworth's new living arrangement did not last long as he ended up returning to Tranby House. 1903 was the year he would find an occupation more beneficial to his community and probably more fulfilling to himself than the occasional charity donation; he decided to become a Justice of the Peace, more commonly known as a magistrate or JP, for the South Hunsley Petty Sessional Division.

A magistrate judged minor criminal cases, such as misdemeanours, criminal damage, assault, public disorder, vagrancy, neighbourly disputes, minor theft and motoring offences. He could also hear cases in the family court and attend to some administrative business, such as granting, renewing and transferring licenses for hotels, inns and pubs. Other duties included analysing applications for ejection of tenants and setting a new scale of fees for solicitors.

JPs usually sit in benches of three, including one chairman or Presiding Justice who speaks on behalf of the other two. Still, they all contribute equally to the final decision. It is not necessary for magistrates to hold any legal qualifications but they are assisted by clerks who do. In the beginning of the 20th century, it was common for the local gentry, major landowners and persons of local consequence to become JPs.[62] So, the fact that Algy chose this new occupation would not have been regarded as extraordinary by any means. He was merely adhering to the status quo of the time.

---

62. Helen Clark, archives supervisor at East Riding of Yorkshire Council, and M. G. Free's personal correspondence with this author.

On 20 October 1903, Barkworth took an oath in which he swore he owned lands, would be faithful to His Majesty King Edward VII, and that he would 'do right to all manner of people...without fear or favour, affection or ill will', and subsequently qualified as a magistrate along with two other men, W. H. Carver and E. S. Wade. (Women were not allowed to serve as magistrates in England until 1919, and the first Black JP would only be appointed in 1962.) As a justice, Algernon was not paid a salary but could receive expenses or loss of earnings payments.[63]

It was not uncommon to have more than three magistrates listening to cases in court. In several sessions, there were four or five (and in one instance up to eight) magistrates hearing cases during petty sessions. The number usually swelled to 20 or more in quarter sessions, traditionally held at four set times each year and reserved for crimes that could not be tried by magistrates without a jury.[64] JPs did not try capital offences, like murder, which were sent to the Court of Assize at York. Barkworth was a part of the Grand Jury once on that court, along with other magistrates, in 1906.[65]

---

63. Algernon's oath courteously provided by Helen Clark, archives supervisor at East Riding of Yorkshire Council; *Driffield Times*, 24 October 1903.

64. Quarter sessions dealt with crimes which were usually too serious for petty sessions but less severe than those tried at the Assize Courts.

65. *Beverley Independent*, 17 March 1906.

Algernon attended the petty sessions every Wednesday[66] in Hull, but the cases for the quarter sessions were heard in Beverley. Job openings from the late 1930s show there was also a monthly session held in the nearby town of Brough.

From 1907 to 1912, the Englishman participated in four petty sessions which took place in the village of Welton, around five miles away from Hessle. According to Helen Clark, archives supervisor for the East Riding of Yorkshire Council, petty sessions were often held wherever they were needed. On those occasions, the magistrate would travel and hear the cases in a public house, the local police station or even a private home. 'There was not often a courthouse as such', she explained.[67] The reasoning behind those sessions taking place at Welton seems to be related to a large number of cases originating from that and other nearby villages. It would be more practical then for the defendants and witnesses to appear at a hearing closer to their homes instead of the more distant city of Hull.

Algernon participated in at least 35 sessions from October 1903 to March 1912 but, as a newcomer, he did not preside over any of them. The most common type of criminal case he tried related to the stealing of money or goods either through theft or burglary. Curiously, the second most usual offence was riding a vehicle (ei-

---

66. Magistrates sometimes met at different days of the week. Since the 1930s, newspapers seemed to have disused the term 'petty sessions', preferring to report that the cases were heard at Hull's East Riding Police Court.

67. Personal correspondence with Helen Clark, archives supervisor at East Riding of Yorkshire Council.

ther a car, bicycle or carriage) without a light at night. In those days, most – if not all – of the lights were not electric, and a candle was used to make sure you were being seen by others on the roads.

As for punishments, most of the cases ended with the defendants serving jail time, followed by fines imposed on the accused, ranging from a mere sixpence to a more considerable five pounds. Time in prison varied between a single day and five years.

Because the JPs dealt mostly with minor offences, some of them can sound amusing nowadays. In October 1906, an elderly man called John Tait was fined 2 shillings, sixpence plus costs for riding a motorcycle without a light in the village of Dunswell. When a constable asked Tait to dismount, he told the officer to 'go to -----' (redacted by the reporter). In court, he explained he thought some boys were shouting at him. Moreover, two young men were fined 11 shillings each in March of the following year for using catapults (a synonym for slingshots) on the highway.[68]

Some cases, though, were much more serious in nature. On 3 April 1906, the court was packed with spectators, anxious to watch the hearing of an 'indecent assault' charge. The defendant was William Whitehead, a member of the County Council, the Beverley Town Council and the Board of Guardians, who had the supposed victim, a girl named Edith Gillyon, in his employ. Whitehead denied the allegations and some witnesses, including his former servants, attested to his 'moral character'. Apparently, and in keeping with the

---

68. *Hull Daily Mail*, 3 October 1906, 28 March 1907, and 9 December 1910.

backward spirit of the times, the young lady was never heard. The jury decided to acquit the accused.[69]

It must have been in court that Algernon met fellow magistrate Henry Harrison-Broadley – they were reported hearing cases together during a quarter session in April 1904. The two became friends and, when Henry decided to run for a House of Commons seat in the 1906 general election, Barkworth backed him. Algy, for instance, occupied the chair of a meeting in support of the Conservative Party politician at Swanland in January 1906. The event was considered 'successful' by the *Hull Daily Mail* and became indeed a forecast of the campaign's outcome: just one month later, Harrison-Broadley was elected.

Four years later, in the December 1910 election, Barkworth would come through again for Henry, lending cars and carriages to transfer Conservative voters from the more isolated districts to the polling booths. Harrison-Broadley benefited from his friend's efforts once more and was re-elected. He would remain a Member of Parliament until his death in 1914.[70]

Outside the courthouse, Algy continued to sit in the lap of luxury. Barkworth's first recorded sea voyage occurred in November 1905, when he joined his older brother, Edmund, his wife, Ada, their three children and the governess, Miss Paqualin, aboard the ship *Tongariro*, owned by The New Zealand Shipping Co., bound for the port of Wellington, the capital of New Zealand. Ada had become ill and her doctors advised a long ocean trip. In that sense, the 70-day-journey

---

69. *The Driffield Times*, 7 April 1906.

70. *Hull Daily Mail*, 5 April 1904, and 22 January 1906.

the *Tongariro* was going to face seemed perfect. There would be layovers in Tenerife (the largest island of the Canary Islands) and Cape Town, South Africa.

They boarded the liner in London and were all travelling in First Class as would be expected. The entire party planned to disembark at Wellington, with the exception of Algy, who decided to accompany them as far as Cape Town. However, that was the port where the voyage ended for the whole family because Ada's condition worsened, and they hurried back home on the first available ship. Ada died after a long illness in February 1912, the year of the JP's next known sea travel.

Algy travelled around England, too, and visited Bath in April 1910. He stayed at the Empire Hotel, an opulent building with six storeys and an octagonal corner tower, and presumably relaxed in the city's famous natural hot springs.

Barkworth's last reported session as a magistrate in early 1912 happened on 20 March. After that, he took a break from his official duties in order to rest. Algy chose the United States, a country he had never visited, as his holiday destination. The Englishman left Hessle on 9 April for London and on the very next day boarded the *Titanic* in Southampton for what he expected to be the trip of a lifetime.[71]

71. Edwards, Brian, *A Swim for Dear Life – The True Story of a Titanic Survivor,* pages 5-6. Courtesy of Bruce Robinson; *Bath Chronicle and Weekly Gazette,* 28 April 1910; *Hull Daily Mail,* 21 March 1912.

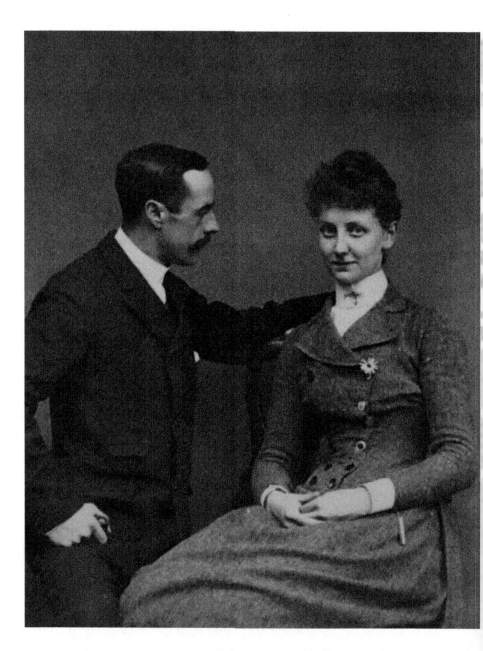

Edmund and Ada Barkworth
(Justin Lowe Collection)

Algy in tweeds, ca. 1904
(Hessle Local History Society Archive)

CHAPTER 4

'You lose your horror
of the dead'

'I cannot recall that I had any sensations as I went down, but when I struck the water it seemed terrifically cold', Algy would later tell of the moment he left the *Titanic* for good and took his chances in the sea. The water temperature that night was only 28º Fahrenheit, which meant the unfortunate people who found themselves struggling in the ocean could have become unconscious in as little as 15 minutes and survived for 45 minutes at most.[72]

The JP submerged with his mouth open, swallowing 'no end of salt water' and spitting out some when his lifejacket brought him back to the surface. He was chilled to the bone but, after swimming for a while, recovered the use of his limbs. The *Titanic* was in her death throes and Barkworth swam away from the vessel with all his strength, fearing the danger of suction. Before he could go far, he was hit on the nose by a plank. 'It put that organ out of use for three days', he

---

72. *Evening Banner*, 26 April 1912; Fitch, Tad, Layton, J. Kent, Wormstedt, Bill, *On a Sea of Glass – The Life & Loss of the RMS Titanic*, page 238.

would remember later. Despite the hard blow, it turned out to be his salvation, because Algy was able to grab onto it and maintain a part of his upper body out of the freezing water. At almost the same time, a huge wave passed over the Englishman's head. That water rush was possibly the result of the *Titanic's* forward funnel crashing down into the ocean.[73]

Barkworth would also be forever grateful for his foresight to wear a fur coat, which, along with the life-jacket and the plank, helped him keep afloat. 'The fur of the coat seemed not to get wet through and retained a certain amount of air that added to buoyancy. I shall never part with it', he declared.

Looking over his shoulder, Algy saw the *Titanic* sinking. But he could not afford to linger, so he continued to swim. Afterwards, Barkworth luckily came across a capsized boat drifting by. It was Collapsible B, which was not launched properly by the *Titanic's* crew and just floated off upside down.

About a dozen men were already clinging to the craft, but there was still room for more. When the magistrate got a hold on the boat, he faced some resistance from its passengers. 'Look out, you will swamp us', some of them said, but Algy took no notice; he knew that boarding the collapsible was his only means of survival.

A short time after climbing onto one of its sides, Barkworth witnessed the *Titanic's* final plunge. He heard three distinct and loud explosions, caused by, in his opinion, air bursting through the decks and the wa-

---

73. *Hull Daily Mail*, 17 May 1912; *Evening Banner*, 26 April 1912; Behe, George, *Titanic Tidbits – Volume 3*, page 172 (unpublished).

tertight compartments succumbing to water pressure. The vessel then broke up in two pieces; the bow settled first, followed by the stern. It was 2.20 a.m. now, and the greatest ship in the world was gone.[74]

After Algy boarded the boat, several other men climbed onto the collapsible until it could hold no more. Aboard were Second Officer Charles Lightoller, Junior Wireless Operator Harold Bride and Chief Baker Charles Joughin as well as First Class passengers Colonel Archibald Gracie and 17-year-old Jack Thayer, one of Barkworth's shipboard acquaintances. At that time, there were more than 30 men on the boat. To make matters worse, sometimes they lost their grip and fell back into the water.

In his book, *The Truth about the Titanic*, Colonel Gracie recalled 'the most tragic crisis' in his life, experienced when the craft had reached its maximum capacity. 'I heard the constant explanation made as we passed men swimming in the wreckage, "Hold on to what you have, old boy; one more of you aboard would sink us all." In no instance, I am happy to say, did I hear any word of rebuke uttered by a swimmer because of refusal to grant assistance. There was no case of cruel violence', he wrote.

Two of Algy's boatmates, situated just behind him, died during the night. One of them fell overboard, but the remaining survivors managed to hang on to the body of the other victim. 'It is extraordinary how under such circumstances you lose your horror of the dead. The death of these two men didn't seem

74. Mowbray, Jay, *Sinking of the Titanic: Thrilling Stories Told by Survivors*, page 183; *Hull Daily Mail*, 17 May 1912.

to make any particular impression upon any of us', he candidly reflected.[75]

If individuals dying on the boat did not upset the JP, the same could not be said about the clamour coming from those struggling in the water. 'I could hear the cries and screams of the drowning people. It was terrible to hear them. We could do nothing for them, for we were helpless on the drifting overturned boat, which was swept away by the strong current from the struggling people in the water. If it had been taken towards them there is no doubt it would have been swamped', he remembered.[76] The current mentioned by Barkworth was the Labrador, which was also responsible for the icebergs drifting further south than expected at that time of the year.

Algy's distressed impressions of the people drowning and freezing in the water were noted by Colonel Gracie in his book: 'The combination of cold and the awful scenes of suffering and death...deeply affected...Mr. R. H. Barkworth [sic], whose tender heart is creditable to his character'.

With no solution in sight for their hardship, those aboard the collapsible turned to spirituality. When someone started cursing, a Catholic seaman intervened. 'This is no time for swearing, it's time to say your prayers. Don't the rest of you think we ought to pray?', he proposed, subsequently inquiring what their boatmates' religious affiliations were. It turns out their lot was quite diverse, with Roman Catholics, Episcopa-

---

75. *Evening Banner*, 26 April 1912; Marshall, Logan, *Sinking of the Titanic and Great Sea Disasters*.

76. *Hull Daily Mail*, 17 May 1912.

lians, Presbyterians and Methodists clinging onto the craft. Algy was Anglican, so either he did not speak up or nobody recalled him doing so. He never mentioned praying in any of his accounts of the disaster.

They then came to an agreement that The Lord's Prayer, also called Our Father, was the most appropriate for all. Leading them was the same crew member who had suggested praying in the first place. 'Our voices with one accord burst forth in repeating that great appeal to the Creator and Preserver of all mankind, and the only prayer that everyone of us knew and could unite in, thereby manifesting that we were all sons of God and brother to each other whatever our sphere in life or creed might be', Gracie poetically described in *The Truth about the Titanic*.

Third Class Survivor Victor Sunderland, one of the first to reach the collapsible, remembered that nearly all of the men aboard were Catholic. Because of that, after the Lord's Prayer, they started saying the Hail Mary, a Catholic prayer. The survivors sang a hymn afterwards.

That entire night, there had been no wind and the sea was placid, allowing a safe evacuation from the sinking ship. All of the Boat B survivors recognized that their craft would certainly founder if the weather conditions worsened, so they continued to pray all night long for the calmness to last.

The men had to crouch beside the boat's keel for lack of space and, as the water was washing up to their waists, their legs were getting numb. To prevent their limbs from freezing and also to attract attention, someone suggested just before sunrise that standing would be a better alternative. 'One by one we stood up very gently, so that our frail craft was not over-balanced.

Even in this position the water washed over our ankles with the least movement', Barkworth remembered later to a newspaper, adding in another interview that all except two of the boat's occupants managed to maintain a nearly erect posture.[77] One of those two might have been Bride, whose legs were immobilized by a man sitting on them.

Daylight brought hope for the *Titanic* survivors, including Boat B's occupants. The men on the upturned collapsible could see, three to five miles distant, the Cunarder *Carpathia*, that had raced about 50 miles[78] to the *Titanic's* rescue. The sighting of another vessel made Algy and others shout loudly with joy. The magistrate noticed, however, that some in the boat were unable to do so; they were nearly frozen and could hardly speak. Unfortunately, the men on the collapsible could do little to nothing in order to propel themselves alongside the *Carpathia*. They had picked up bits of wood, but these rudimentary tools were practically ineffective in getting closer.[79]

The only means of rescue would be to transfer to another – right-side up – lifeboat. Lightoller saw to this

77. *Hull Daily Mail*, 17 May 1912; *Evening Banner*, 26 April 1912; *New York Times*, 19 April 1912; Gracie, Archibald, Thayer, Jack, *Titanic: A Survivor's Story & The Sinking of the S. S. Titanic*, page 97; *Cleveland Plain Dealer*, 26 April 1912; American Inquiry, page 995; Hyslop, Donald, Forsyth, Alastair, Jemima, Sheila, *Titanic Voices*, page 152.

78. Dave Gittins' recalculation, published on the book *Report Into the Loss of the SS Titanic*, page 177.

79. American Inquiry, pages 76 and 786; *The New York Times*, 19 April 1912.

by using his whistle, calling the attention of Boats 4 and 12 half a mile away. They had been part of a mini flotilla that night, along with lifeboats 10, 14 and Collapsible D. 'Come over and take us off', the officer shouted. 'Aye, aye; I am coming over', Able Bodied Seaman Frederick Clench, in Boat 12, answered. The two lifeboats cast off from the others and rowed directly to Collapsible B.

As it was too dark to see anything until then, this was the first moment Algy noticed one of the *Titanic's* officers was aboard the craft. He also recognized his shipboard acquaintance, teenager Jack Thayer, clinging to Boat B with him. In his 1940 account of the disaster, Thayer mentions Barkworth as one of the passengers aboard Boat B but says nothing else about the Englishman.

It was a timely rescue; the ocean, which had been as smooth as glass, had now become choppy due to a strong breeze. It caused the upturned craft, already low in the water, to roll around, making the air leave its interior and the boat to sink at a faster pace. The water was creeping in and had already reached the men's knees. Lightoller, clearly in charge, directed the survivors to face one way and lean to one side or the other to preserve the boat's remaining buoyancy and also so the men could maintain their foothold on the slippery planks, by then well underwater.

All aboard knew that death would be swift should they fail to keep the air pocket inside Collapsible B. 'Had the boat been completely turned over, compelling us to cling to the submerged gunwale, it could not have supported our weight, and we should have been frozen to death in the ice-cold water before rescue could reach us', Gracie hypothesized in his book.[80]

Following Lightoller's orders, the men clambered into lifeboats 4 and 12 in perfect order, beginning at one end of Boat B and finishing at the other. Any mad dash would mean unbalancing the collapsible and dumping the others into the water. 'I never felt so happy as when I got in it [Boat 12] and felt I was safe', Algy remembered.[81] Around 28 to 30 men are thought to have been rescued from Collapsible B by the two lifeboats.[82]

As Lightoller related in his book, *Titanic and Other Ships*, written more than two decades after the sinking: 'However anyone that had sought refuge on that upturned Engleheart [actually Engelhardt, the kind of the collapsible boats used on the *Titanic*] survived the night is nothing short of miraculous. If ever human endurance was taxed to the limit, surely it was during those long hours of exposure in a temperature below

80. Gracie, Archibald, Thayer, Jack, *Titanic: A Survivor's Story & The Sinking of the S. S. Titanic*, page 94; American Inquiry, page 639; Lightoller, Charles, *Titanic and Other Ships*, pages 129-130.

81. *Hull Daily Mail*, 17 May 1912; *The New York Times*, 19 April 1912.

82. Although all survivors rescued from Collapsible B were men, and some of its occupants declared only men were ever aboard it, there might have been women and children holding onto the boat at first. Third Class survivor Eugene Daly told Dr Frank Blackmarr, a Carpathia passenger, that men, women and children gradually slid from Collapsible B into the water. Third Class survivor Edward Dorkings, who is thought to have been aboard Boat B, remembered a woman on the Collapsible (*Bureau County Republican*, 2 May 1912). If they were right, then these unknown ladies and children unfortunately did not make it through the night.

freezing, standing motionless in our wet clothes. That the majority were still standing when the first faint streaks of dawn appeared is proof that whilst there is life there is still some hope'.

Collapsible B, on which Algy stood in the early hours of 15 April 1912, was found some days later by the Mackay-Bennett, a ship hired by White Star Line to recover the bodies of the Titanic's victims (Ioannis Georgiou Collection)

Barkworth ended up in Boat 12, which, according to his calculation, had 60 people aboard after the transfer. In reality, it dangerously held 69 occupants, four more than its maximum capacity. Besides the living, the body of the man who had died on Collapsible B also found its way into the lifeboat. The corpse was brought to the *Carpathia* and subsequently became one of four *Titanic* victims who were buried at sea from the rescue ship. His identity has been the subject of debate for a long time, but recent research shows he was most likely Third Class passenger David Livshin.[83]

Algy found some relief when a woman in the lifeboat kindly gave him a steamer rug, which he shared with Gracie and a crew member, possibly a fireman. 'The steamer rug was a great comfort as we drew it over our heads and huddled close together to obtain some warmth', said the colonel in his book. While testifying at the American inquiry which investigated the *Titanic* disaster, Gracie revealed that Barkworth, as a bald man, was very grateful for this protection. 'It was very grateful to me, too', Archibald added.[84]

Overcrowded as it was, Boat 12's gunwales now settled very low above the surface of the water, and it moved slowly across the now rough ocean. Lightoller assumed the command of the lifeboat and steered the tiller at the stern. The officer's recollections years later would reveal that Boat 12 was not as safe as Algy thought it was:

---

83. For more on the *Titanic* bodies recovered by the *Carpathia*, please see Appendix P, 'Buried at Sea', from *On a Sea of Glass – The Life & Loss of the RMS Titanic* by Tad Fitch, J. Kent Layton and Bill Wormstedt.

84. American Inquiry, page 997.

'Sea and wind were rising. Every wave threatened to come over the bows of our overloaded lifeboat and swamp us. All were women and children in the boat apart from those of us men from the Engleheart [sic]. Fortunately, none of them realised how near we were to being swamped.

I trimmed the boat down a little more by the stern, and raised the bow, keeping her carefully bow on to the sea, and hoping against hope she would continue to rise. Sluggishly, she lifted her bows, but there was no life in her with all that number on board.

Then, at long last, the Carpathia *definitely turned her head towards us, rounding to about 100 yards to windward. Now to get her safely alongside! We couldn't last many minutes longer, and round the* Carpathia's *bows was a scurry of wind and waves that looked like defeating my efforts after all. One sea lapped over the bow, and the next one far worse. The following one she rode, and then, to my unbounded relief, she came through the scurry into calm water under the* Carpathia's *lee'.*[85]

---

85. Lightoller, Charles, *Titanic and Other Ships*, page 130.

At 8.15 a.m., Boat 12 was the last lifeboat to be picked up by the *Carpathia*. Barkworth witnessed women being sent up the side of the vessel in slings and children in coal bags. The men, on the other hand, had to climb up a rope ladder, a task which the magistrate found difficult after the experience the Boat B's men had gone through, and because of the rolling of the ship. Climbing must have been extra hard for him because his hands were frozen after swimming in the cold water hours earlier. Despite the difficulty, Algy made do and was saved at last.

He did not record for posterity much of his activities on the Cunarder but mentioned that the survivors were treated with great hospitality. 'No words of mine can speak too highly of the kindness of the captain, officers, doctors, and crew alike', Barkworth said. The justice became a member of a survivors committee while aboard, along with fellow First Class passengers Samuel Goldenberg, Frederic Spedden, William Carter, Frederic Seward, Isaac Frauenthal, Karl Behr, Margaret Brown and Mauritz Björnström-Steffansson.

They all signed a small note of appreciation addressed to the captain of the *Carpathia*, Arthur Rostron, its officers and passengers. 'On behalf of the survivors of the *Titanic* we desire to express to each and all our heartfelt thanks for the kindness of treatment and full-hearted welcome accorded us on board your ship. It will be our sincere endeavour to express our thanks at an appropriate and fitting manner at the earliest possible moment', said the text.[86]

---

86. *Hull Daily Mail*, 17 May 1912; Behe, George, *Voices From the Carpathia – Rescuing RMS Titanic*.

The survivors committee also set up an aid fund to attend to the needs of those who had lost everything in the disaster. By 19 April, around 10,000 dollars (about $280,755 today) were collected, Algy being among the subscribers.[87] Although he later claimed all his cash had been in his dispatch case, which by then was lying on the ocean floor, Algy probably had a small sum with him, allowing the JP to contribute to the cause. He was a Barkworth, after all, and philanthropy was in his DNA.

The Englishman's frozen hands would certainly have been treated by the *Carpathia*'s doctor, Frank McGhee, who was responsible for taking care of First Class survivors' ailments. Maybe he even checked Barkworth's injured nose. During the journey to the United States, Algy dictated his first account of the sinking to *Carpathia* passenger Mr Cecil R. Francis. He could not write due to the state of his hands.

The magistrate was also able to send at least three Marconigrams to alert his family back in England that he was still alive. One of them was addressed to his elderly mother, Catherine, who had been staying at the resort town of Scarborough, some 38 miles from Hessle. The message, received on the afternoon of 15 April, contained the word 'Safe' and apparently nothing else, which might not have been the best idea since Mrs Barkworth and other relatives wondered if it had been sent before the sinking. To the family in Hessle, Algy chose less ambiguous words for a telegram sent

---

87. *New York Times*, 20 April 1912; Calculation made through *US Inflation Calculation*. Link: https://www.usinflationcalculator.com/, visited on 31 December 2021.

three days later, to their relief: 'Am safe on board *Carpathia*'. He followed this with another cablegram on 19 April, emphasizing his survival and well-being.

The Marconigram Barkworth sent on the 18th survives to this day. It went up for auction in July 2021, along with another message from Harold Cottam, the *Carpathia*'s wireless operator. Cottam was asking for instructions in order to cope with the 'enormous rush of work' that arose after the *Titanic* collision. The two messages were sold for $3,804.

Carpathia's Marconigram that Algy sent to his family at Hessle (RR Auction)

Algy's 18 April message was the ultimate piece of evidence the Barkworths needed to convince themselves of his survival, but it had not been the first. Regional newspapers such as the *Yorkshire Evening Post* had already published in their 16 April edition that 'A. H. Barkworth' was among the passengers saved from the wreck.

This information was obtained in a very indirect manner. Cottam was working restlessly to transmit the list of survivors to Cape Race, on the island of Newfoundland, the nearest point of land that their equipment could reach. Cape Race then relayed the names to New York, where they were picked up by news agencies. Telegrams from the Reuters agency containing the updated list were afterwards sent across the Atlantic Ocean to London and found their way into the newspapers on the 16th, many of them running special extra editions to inform their readers of the tragedy.

However, those lists did contain inaccuracies, going as far as misidentifying survivors as victims and vice-versa. Reuters clarified that 'the confusion in some of the names is due to interruption by amateur wireless telegraphists'. Indeed, Algy's name was one of several to be misspelled by the papers: the *Daily Mirror* listed him as 'A. N. Barkworth' on 17 April. That kind of error might have left the family doubtful regarding the justice's safety, which would finally be confirmed by the 18 April telegram.[88]

---

88. *Evening Banner*, 26 April 1912; *Northern Daily Mail*, 17 April 1912, courtesy of Randy Bryan Bigham; *The Yorkshire Post*, 19 April 1912, courtesy of Randy Bryan Bigham; *Hull Daily Mail*, 19 April 1912; *Yorkshire Evening Post*, 16 April 1912; *Westminster Gazette*, 16 April 1912; *Daily Mirror*, 17 April 1912.

It appears that Algy's hands at least partially healed while he was still aboard the *Carpathia*, evidenced by a postcard of the ship that he used to pen a second, shorter account of the disaster. 'Put on *Carpathia* on the morning of 15 April 1912 ex[89] *'Titanic'* which sank at 2.20 a.m. lat: 41.06 West long: 5.14. Jumped overboard and got on to an overturned boat until rescued', he wrote.[90]

While on the *Carpathia*, Barkworth also gave some personal information for the ship's manifest. Besides his full name, age and occupation, Algy strangely stated his nearest relative was a certain 'W. Ellum', from 5 Parliament Street, 'Hessel'[91]; that he had never been in the United States before; was not a polygamist nor an anarchist; had never been to prison; and that he was in good health. The document also provided some data on the magistrate's physical appearance: he was 5' 9'', had a Mediterranean complexion, brown hair and blue eyes.

---

89. A preposition which means 'from'. Algy meant he became a *Carpathia* passenger after the sinking of the *Titanic*.

90. Edwards, Brian, *A Swim for Dear Life – The True Story of a Titanic Survivor*, page 18. Courtesy of Bruce Robinson.

91. Actually, 5 Parliament Street is located in Hull, and, according to researcher Justin Lowe, it housed (and still houses) lawyers and solicitors' offices. 'W. Ellum', a possible misspelling, may have been one of Algy's legal advisors. This theory is backed up by the fact that his lawyer in the '40s, Harold Edward Jackson, also worked from that same address.

Four postcards from Algy: two were sent to Edmund and Dorothy while he was still on the Titanic; one is blank; and another, from Carpathia, contains his short Titanic account (Hessle Local History Society Archive)

Algy luckily got to sleep in a stateroom aboard the *Carpathia*, which makes one wonder why he did not renounce it in favour of some of the hundreds of women survivors who were forced to rest in the ship's public rooms due to lack of space. The *Carpathia* was a small ship compared to the *Titanic* and had only 75% of the enormous White Star liner's passenger capacity. Instead, Barkworth had the company of a young Londoner from Second Class – 19-year-old William Mellors. The pair became somewhat intimate, because they met at least once on dry land.[92]

After the *Carpathia* docked at Pier 54 in New York on the rainy night of 18 April 1912, Algy went straight to the fashionable Imperial Hotel, located at the intersection of Broadway and 32nd Street. He carried only a small bundle of clothing that was given to him on the rescue ship.

'Can you take me in?', asked Barkworth. 'I was a passenger on the *Titanic*. I haven't any money', he explained. Perhaps he had given all he had left to the survivors committee. 'Make yourself at home, and if you want anything ask for it', was the clerk's answer; other luxury hotels in the area were also willing to give free accommodation to the *Titanic* survivors. The Breslin was one of those, and even sent a member of its staff to the pier in order to offer its services, especially for Second Class passengers. But, at least on that night, none of the 712 survivors took up the Breslin's offer.

---

92. Barkworth and Mellors were not the only male passengers to have slept in a cabin on the *Carpathia*. Bruce Ismay was voluntarily confined to a cabin during the entire trip to New York, and Colonel Archibald Gracie also admitted, in his book *The Truth about the Titanic*, to having a cabin.

After checking in at the Imperial, the JP's first request was a toothbrush, which was promptly fulfilled by a bellboy. Before he retired, Barkworth was interviewed by a reporter from *The New York Times*, who noted the magistrate was in a nervous condition and his hands were still in bad shape, but otherwise he seemed unscathed by the tragedy.

Algy agreed to share his account of the disaster with the journalist but showed signs of exhaustion when asked about the events that took place after his rescue. 'I cannot go into the details of the scenes among the survivors on the *Carpathia*. I want to forget it all for a time and get a long night's sleep', he vented, implying the atmosphere aboard the Cunarder was one of sorrow and despair.[93]

The Englishman stayed at the hotel until at least the morning of 24 April (by then, perhaps his family had wired him money to pay his bill), when he was interviewed in the lobby by another reporter. Algy was patiently smoking a pipe while waiting to talk with Mellors, who was also staying at the same hotel. Probably the pair went to the Imperial together on the 18th.

Barkworth told the journalist the young man was still suffering the effects of the sinking after having to swim for his life that night: he had a frozen foot and the ankle of his other leg was seriously injured. Mellors had been swept away from the *Titanic* by a wave that hit the Boat Deck and survived by climbing aboard Collapsible A, which, like Collapsible B, had not been properly launched and was washed off the ship. Boat A was right-side up, unlike B, but its canvas sides could

---

93. *Evening Banner*, 26 April 1912; *The New York Times*, 19 April 1912, and 20 April 1912.

William Mellors befriended Algy on the Carpathia and
the two stayed at the Imperial Hotel afterwards; he is
seen here in a 1919 passport photo (National Archives
and Records Administration)

not be pulled up, so its passengers had to endure standing all night with water up to their knees.

William had saved a little money to better his life in the United States but had lost everything on the *Titanic*. Algy was looking after Mellors, trying to find him a job before returning to England - at least one newspaper remarked how the justice had been 'particularly kind' to the Londoner. Unfortunately, the journalist did not describe how the survivors' meeting went,[94] but the pair did give a joint interview most likely during the time they were at the Imperial. It has been published in the books *Sinking of the Titanic and Great Sea Disasters*, edited by Logan Marshall, and *Sinking of the Titanic – Thrilling Stories Told by Survivors*, edited by Jay Mowbray.

During his stay at the hotel, presumably on 21 April, Algy sent a cable to the *Hull Daily Mail*, giving a brief account of his survival. He would have to clarify this message later, which he wrote in a hurry:

'Please announce Algernon Barkworth, Hessle, arrived New York on *Carpathia*, ex *Titanic* sank. Jumped into sea, drop 30 feet, just before she sank. Swam clear, and saw *Titanic* sink. Cold intense. Held on to overturned boat for six hours. Picked up eventually by one of *Titanic*'s boats. Suffering from frost-bitten fingers.

A H. Barkworth'[95]

---

94. *The Yorkshire Post*, 27 April 1912; *Evening Banner*, 26 April 1912.

95. *Hull Daily Mail*, 22 April 1912.

Algy's portrait, which was published by some
newspapers during the Titanic sinking's coverage
(Hessle Local History Society Archive)

Meanwhile, the English press was angling for any information about the disaster and its survivors and victims. Barkworth was the subject of several of these news stories. One of them described him as 'a young man of independent means'.[96]

Algy, at 47, was by no means a young man at the time. But of more importance was the expression 'of independent means'. This is a euphemism, indicating his source of income was money he inherited or earned from investments rather than a job. As a member of the English upper class and of a wealthy and traditional family, he could indulge in not pursuing a professional career. And he was not the only Barkworth to have been defined as such; census forms described his mother, Catherine, his sister Evelyn and himself as living on their own – or private – means. So, from where exactly was the JP's money coming? It is likely Algy was a shareholder in the family businesses, and he was listed as being the owner of a dozen ships in 1909. Later in life, Barkworth also may have had interests in the Reckitt and Sons company because he was present at its annual meetings from 1935 to 1937.[97]

Algy would not go back home right away. From New York, he travelled approximately 180 miles to the small town of Concord, Massachusetts, where he stayed in Mrs Richard F. Wood's home as a guest until

---

96. *Scarborough Mercury*, 19 April 1912.

97. Free, M. G., *Algernon Henry Barkworth*, page 1, Hull History Centre Records (unpublished); *Hull Daily Mail*, 26 April 1935, 1 May 1936, and 30 April 1937. Reckitt and Sons was a Hull-based manufacturer of household products, notably starch, black lead, laundry blue and household polish.

the end of the month. Possibly, this is where he had planned to go on holiday all along.

However, Barkworth would find no rest there due to the recent trauma he had suffered. He told his hostess that this first trip to the United States would probably be his last. 'It was a terrible experience, some of it so horrible that he is endeavouring to efface it from his memory...Although a strong, vigorous man, the terrible strain has told severely on him and he shows the intense suffering which has been his', one newspaper wrote of the Englishman's state of mind.

Mrs Wood took Algy sightseeing one day in a possible attempt to distract him from his recent predicament. They visited several parts of the town, including the famous Old North Bridge, the location of the 'shot heard round the world'. It was there that the American War of Independence started, on the morning of 19 April 1775, when hundreds of Colonial Minutemen exchanged gunfire with British army troops. But long-ago fought battles were something the survivor's mind could not yet process. Looking down on the historic bridge, all Barkworth could see was the Concord River's 'treacherous water'. His thoughts seemed to linger on the horrors he witnessed during, and mainly after, the foundering of the *Titanic*.

He declared to the local press he did not wish to remain in America any longer due to his nervous condition and sailed back to England on 30 April. It can only be speculated if this new sea crossing, only two weeks after the sinking, disturbed him further. After arriving safely in his home country, Algy spent some time paying visits in the south of England, including in London.

Around this time, he wrote to Edith Gee, his friend Arthur Gee's widow. The letter is in possession of his great-grandson Martin Gee. Although it is currently in storage, Martin remembers its content well. Apparently, Algy's goal in contacting Edith was to provide an account of her husband's last hours alive.

'He [Algy] wrote how he sat with Gee and another [Charles Jones] in the smoking room and they observed some men playing cards in the same room. Gee disapproved', Martin said. 'When the iceberg was hit, they felt a slight judder and went out onto the deck. After putting on their cork jackets, they stood by the rail of the ship waiting. The bow took a dive and Algernon jumped, leaving Gee standing on the rail. He wrote how his fingers still suffered from the cold of that night and didn't work properly'. After he was done visiting, Barkworth returned to Hessle in mid-May.[98]

Sought after by the local press, the JP gave yet another account of the *Titanic* disaster. He took this opportunity to clarify the hasty cable he had sent to the *Hull Daily Mail* informing family and friends of his survival. As his wording might have given the impression he was immersed in the ocean for six hours, he explained that would have been a physical impossibility because of the coldness of the water.

Algy added that he had practically recovered from his trying experience although his fingers were still a little stiff. 'He is being overwhelmed with congratulations and inquiries. A sad side consists of the commu-

98. *Concord Enterprise*, 1 May 1912; *Hull Daily Mail*, 2 May 1912; *American Register*, 19 May 1912; Martin Gee's personal correspondence with this author.

nications he is receiving from relatives asking for news of those who never returned. Of course he is unable to answer them', concluded the news story.[99]

Postcard showing Old North Bridge, above Concord River, whose 'treacherous water' impressed Algy (Author's Collection)

---

99. *Hull Daily Mail*, 17 May 1912.

CHAPTER 5

The councilman and the chauffeur

Back in his homeland, Barkworth was ready to start a new chapter of his life. And what better way not to dwell on his near-death experience than to take up a new activity? Maybe that was the reason behind his announcement to run for a vacant seat on the East Riding County Council (division of Hessle and Anlaby) almost as soon as he arrived in England.

Algernon had a contender for the post, a solicitor named W. C. Dawson, but it appears the magistrate already started the campaign with the upper hand. 'Mr Barkworth has manifest qualifications for the position, and we understand that he will be very strongly and enthusiastically supported', wrote the *Hull Daily Mail* on 13 May 1912. He had several connections all over the region, and it could not hurt his case that he was now nationally known as a *Titanic* survivor.

Dawson might have sensed he was going to be defeated, because he withdrew his candidacy a few days after Barkworth showed interest in the job. Dawson's reason for the press was that he, the chairman of the Hull Education Committee and the Hessle Urban Council, had found out he would have to take on responsibilities 'in other directions...where the needs are greatest, and not where the honours are highest', thus preventing him from continuing to run. With Dawson out of the way, Algernon was successfully elected County Councillor on 16 May.

His first act in his new position was to announce his purposes as a councilman. 'I beg to assure you that I shall at all times devote myself to the best interests of the electors and do all in my power for the benefit of the parishes of Hessle and Anlaby. I also wish to tender my sincere thanks to my Committee for the large amount of work they had done in such a short time, and I feel sure that had the contest taken place, the results of their efforts would have been apparent', he wrote in the *Daily Mail* the day after his election.[100]

Barkworth acted as a councillor for several years. In this new position, it would be his duty to debate and decide on matters related to road maintenance, disease outbreaks, the construction or alteration of buildings, water supplies, medical examinations of children, cottages for labourers and old age pension claims, among others.

The advent of World War I in July 1914 considerably changed the issues dealt with by Algernon both as a councillor and as a magistrate. In the former, he had to handle situations such as 107 windows from the local asylum that were badly shaded, a problem discussed during a session in November 1915. This was important during war-time periods because curtains prevented inside lights from being seen by enemy aircraft, making air raids more difficult. The possibility

---

100. *Hull Daily Mail*, 16 May 1912, and 17 May 1912.

of obtaining voluntary recruits among teachers was also analysed on the same occasion.

Barkworth resumed his activities as a Justice of the Peace in June 1912, less than two months after his return to England. He was reported for the first time as presiding at a session in March 1914, when he, along with colleague Colonel Wellsted (a neighbour of his), judged a woman's plea for separation after her husband had left her with a son to raise. The request was granted by the magistrates, who also demanded that the man pay maintenance of 10 shillings a week on behalf of his child.[101]

Algernon's second time in the chair took place three months later, during which he heard a case that concealed more twists and turns than an Agatha Christie novel. A woman named Christina Dales accused John William Stabler of assaulting her son Edward, who was only seven years old. In court, the boy described that Stabler 'laid him on his knee and smacked him five or six times', including in the face.

The plot thickened when Edward was questioned about the reason for Stabler to commit such a heinous act. The boy confessed to, some time before, throwing lime in the eyes of John's son, Albert, aged only four. Because of this, the child was hospitalized for two months, had to wear glasses and was in danger of having one of his eyes removed. To make matters worse, the day before his beating, Edward threw stones at Albert, who had been recently released from the hospital. The victim had been proven to be a bully.

---

101. *Hull Daily Mail*, 25 March 1914.

'You ought to be very thankful you had somebody to thrash the boy', the court's clerk, T. L. Locking, said to Mrs Dales, verbalizing what perhaps everybody in the room was thinking. 'Yes, sir, but it is not the first time [Stabler hit Edward]', answered the woman. She surprisingly added she had 'horsewhipped the boy until he could not stand', possibly after the lime episode; Stabler's punishment seems to pale in comparison to the blows Edward's own mother inflicted on him. This being such a convoluted case, Barkworth and fellow magistrate J. M. Wares thought best to dismiss it. Unfortunately, the newspapers did not record what Algernon thought of the whole situation.[102]

The next time he would preside over a session would be in the midst of WWI, in June 1915, when he heard a case regarding an unshaded light. It came from the attic of a fellow Hull justice, John Watt, who claimed the room in question was utilized as servants' quarters. They did not follow his instructions about not letting any lights show and were fired as a result. 'We are obliged to record a conviction against you, but we wish to state that we do not believe you had an intention of contravening the regulations',[103] said Algernon, perhaps to mitigate the situation with his colleague, who was fined 10 shillings.

On the same occasion, the Bench also fined Ernest Macdonald 30 shillings for similar reasons: he was driving a motor car whose lights shone too bright-

---

102. *Hull Daily Mail*, 10 June 1914.

103. Possible reference to the UK Defence of the Realm Act passed in 1914 after the outbreak of the war; *Hull Daily Mail*, 2 June 1915.

ly and, after being stopped by the police, failed to produce his license. 'In imposing this fine, the Chairman of the Bench [Barkworth] remarked that it was the duty of everyone at the present time to comply with the new regulations', the *Hull Daily Mail* wrote.[104]

Algernon would act as chairman again only a week later. The offence once more concerned a breach of wartime rules: three young men were caught using a flashlight at 10.40 p.m. This time, however, he was more lenient, declaring the magistrates were 'inclined to look mercifully on the case, and regard it as an error of judgment on the part of the defendants'. Barkworth advised them to remain indoors at night and dismissed the case.

This might have been the justice's only controversial ruling, given the fact that the *Hull Daily Mail* started receiving letters about the magistrates' decision soon after that session. They were written by citizens who believed the men ought to have stayed in custody of the police and its officers should have been allowed to continue their inquiries. Barkworth also headed a session, in September 1916, in which three men were fined for not obscuring interior lights.[105]

The concern over unshaded lights was justified since Hull was the target of at least eight Zeppelin raids during the war, from 1915 to 1918, causing the deaths of over 160 people. German bombs and explosives also sparked raging fires and damaged many buildings,

---

104. *Hull Daily Mail*, 2 June 1915.

105. *Hull Daily Mail*, 11 June 1915, 12 June 1915, and 20 September 1916.

including the Holy Trinity Church, which Algernon attended.[106] Its stained-glass windows melted during the first attack, on 6 June 1915, but the building survived. Hull was frequently chosen as a target because its location, on the British east coast, could be easily reached by air from the north-western German coast.

In a quarter session that took place in October 1915, a thief who stole money and goods from a house was discharged by Algernon and the other justices. The Bench was 'very unwilling' to send him to prison because he was a soldier and due to his superior officer speaking on his behalf in court. Nevertheless, other soldiers who committed more serious crimes – such as sexual assault – ended up being sentenced to hard labour by Barkworth and the rest of the Bench. And one previously convicted private who had stolen a watch was sentenced to two months in prison.[107]

Algernon's animal expertise came in handy in a case he presided over about a year later, in December 1916. Two men, Alfred Jackson and Robert Towse, were summoned for making a debilitated mare drive a wagon. It had an injury on its knee which caused the animal great pain, according to a veterinary surgeon's testimony.

Barkworth must have been extremely interested in the outcome of this particular hearing because the JP did something he had never done before and would never do again: he actually left the premises of the

106. Algy was also a parishioner of All Saints' Church in Hessle, which still exists.

107. *Hull Daily Mail*, 19 October 1915, and 20 December 1916.

courthouse to have a look at the beast and, on returning, declared he had never seen a horse in such a bad
state and could not understand how any man with a
conscience could have taken a horse out in that condition. Being so keen on animals, Algernon must have
been appalled and shocked by the abuse the mare had
had to endure. Jackson and Towse were fined 50 shillings for their transgression, and the poor horse had
to be put down.[108]

The magistrate supported the war effort: he donated £5 for the Hull Recruiting Committee's out-
of-pocket expenses in September 1914 and £1 1s two
months later on behalf of the Blue Cross Fund for
Horses at the Front. Its aim was to treat injured animals – of which Barkworth was very fond. He even
donated a fat pig (weighing about 12 stone) for a Red
Cross Fund sale.[109]

It was during the military conflict that Algy lost
his mother. Catherine died on 29 August 1915, age 77.
Several family members and friends accompanied her
funeral three days later, including her four children,
Edmund's daughter Dorothy, former Tranby House
governess Amelia Coxhead, and Rose Ann Roper,
a companion to Catherine. In her obituary, Algy's
mother was described as being respected by the entire Hessle community and 'a most charitable lady'.[110]

---

108. *Hull Daily Mail*, 06 December 1916.

109. *Hull Daily Mail*, 05 September 1914, 12 November 1914, and
21 December 1915.

110. *Hull Daily Mail*, 31 August 1915, courtesy of Justin Lowe;
Yorkshire Post and Leeds Intelligencer, 2 September 1915.

Algy was one of the executors of his mother's will. She left an estate valued at £17,121 2s (almost £1,4 million pounds currently). Edmund and Algernon received £1,000 pounds each, while her daughters, Violet and Evelyn, were willed the remainder of her property. She was very generous towards the staff of Tranby House, leaving money to her butler, William Thorne, and gardener, George Firth, for instance. Miss Roper received £200, and the same amount was bequeathed to the other executor, Harold Pease (her son-in-law, husband of her daughter Violet).[111]

Legally, Edmund, the older brother, was to have inherited Tranby House but he had already made a life of his own elsewhere. He had been a partner of the family company, Barkworth & Spaldin, which his father, Henry, managed until 1888, when it was taken over by Thorpe, Balfour & Harrison. After this, Edmund seemed to have lost interest in the business. He married Clara Reid in 1890 and moved to a farming estate he had inherited in the village of Piddletrenthide, in Dorset County. Besides tending to his crops, he also became a barrister. But Edmund did not merely hand over the mansion to his younger brother; Algy reputedly had to pay £4,000 for it.[112]

---

111. *Hull Daily Mail*, 30 October 1915.

112. Free, M. G., *The House of Barkworth*, pages 8 and 12, Hessle Local History Society, 2016 (unpublished); Elverson, John, *The Barkworth Family*, page 16 (unpublished); Edwards, Brian, *A Swim for Dear Life – The True Story of a Titanic Survivor*, page 20. Courtesy of Bruce Robinson.

Catherine Barkworth
(Justin Lowe Collection)

Not all was tragic in Barkworth's life, though. After his *Titanic* experience, he kept himself busy not only with work but with the social events he enjoyed so much. The magistrate was already active in his community again by 20 July 1912, when a horse show took place in Brough, a small town near Hessle. His spirits seemed to be up because he wished the contest success and complimented its 'all-round excellence'. He took the second and third prizes on the 'roadster gelding or mare driven in harness' and the 'roadster gelding or mare' categories, respectively.[113]

A mere five days later, Algy was brushing up on the political situation at a meeting of the Hull branch of the Howdenshire Conservative and Unionist Association, whose reunions he would attend regularly in following years. In February 1915, at one of these meetings, he voted for Stanley Jackson to fill the House of Commons' vacant spot left by the death of Henry Harrison-Broadley, of whom Barkworth had also shown support years before. Jackson, Harrison-Broadley's son-in-law, was the only candidate for the position and ended up occupying it until he resigned his seat in 1926. For his turn, the substitute was also approved by Algy; Major William Carver was not only a member of the Conservative Party but a Justice of the Peace, too. Carver faced Liberal candidate Frederick Linfield and came out victorious, keeping his seat until 1945. Barkworth was one of the most important members of the Hull and Hessle divisions of the

113. *Hull Daily Mail*, 22 July 1912.

Association, reaching the vice-president position in both of them.[114]

As his enthusiasm during the July horse show demonstrated, his love for animals had not diminished. Algy reserved much of his time tending to the animals he possessed. He continued to buy and sell horses, bulls and cows, sheep and poultry. The Englishman advertised the sale of pullets, cocks and cockerels of the 'best breed and quality' in the *Hull Daily Mail* in February 1917 and for the first time gave his Tranby House address for people interested in checking out the birds.[115]

The mystery of Stanley House

When Algernon advertised some Silver Campine Cockerels for sale in September 1914, he gave as his address a certain 'Stanley House' in Hessle. According to Michael Free, in correspondence with this author, the Barkworths did own other properties, mostly cottages, and some of them were occupied by servants or estate workers. The Barkworths were regarded as good landlords and provided better houses to their farm hands than other employers. Stanley House might have been one of them, although Free has never found any evidence of such a place ever existing in Hessle.

---

114. *Hull Daily Mail*, 26 July 1912; *Yorkshire Post and Leeds Intelligencer*, 11 February 1915.

115. *Hull Daily Mail*, 19 February 1917.

On the other hand, Justin Lowe believes Stanley House is the result of a typo and that the birds were actually being sold at Tranby House. 'Tranby and Stanley sound quite similar. Possibly the advert was telephoned and Tranby could have been taken for Stanley. Tranby isn't a very usual word unless you know it. I'm certain it's a mistake; I don't think he'd have owned another big property and kept chickens at it', he theorized in a personal message to this author. Lowe's hypothesis does not explain, however, why the exact same advert was published in three different editions of the Hull Daily Mail *(September 29th, September 30th and October 1st), without any corrections whatsoever.*

This indicates the JP no longer confined his animals to the Swanland farm and they were now kept at his main house as well. It is possible this change happened after Catherine's death, when Algy became the mansion's new owner. Besides fowl, there were dogs, pigs, bulls, cows, horses, donkeys and at least one cat living the good life at Tranby.

Barkworth started burying his most beloved deceased animals on the house's grounds and soon a pet cemetery was established. It would remain on the property for decades. According to Justin Lowe, Algy had at least six dogs during his lifetime: four red Chow-Chows named Peter, Paul, Nancy and Noa, and two smaller dogs, perhaps Jack Russell Terriers.[116] He

---

116. Justin Lowe's personal correspondence with this author.

also possessed prized Chow-Chows, which competed in dog shows.

Probably some or all of these animals lived on the property's 'home farm', which boasted barns and a 3-stall stable on its 31.650-acre grounds. It shared boundaries with Barrow Lane, Ferriby Road and Heads Lane, the original name of the street where Tranby House stands. Barkworth must have dedicated a lot of his time and attention to this large area because on the 1921 Census he declared himself to be a work-at-home 'gentleman farmer' - his JP position was written down but later crossed out.

There was at least one occasion when Algy's animals caused some distress among the community. Two Hessle butchers had bought two bullocks from Barkworth, and in the early hours of a 1926 December morning, they arrived at Tranby House to collect them. The bulls, however, broke away from their field and ran madly along a road that led to the village of Swanland. Perhaps they were trying to reach Easenby Farm.

The beasts left a path of destruction behind them. 'Passing Hessle Mount at a furious rate, they cut across fields towards Tranby Croft,[117] taking hedges in their stampede. Turning down towards Anlaby [a nearby village], they broke into a field where they galloped up and down for a considerable time', the *Hull Daily Mail* reported. The butchers spent all day trying to recover the bullocks, only succeeding shortly before nightfall.[118]

---

117. Hessle Mount and Tranby Croft are mansions near Tranby House which still stand today.

118. *Hull Daily Mail*, 18 December 1926.

*Equines grazing next to Tranby House
(top – Author's Collection /
bottom - Hessle Local History Society Archive)*

*Algy (right) sits on a fence with brother Edmund and
nephew Henry in the early 1900s
(John Elverson Collection)*

Tranby House servants pose next to a donkey in the early 1900s (Hessle Local History Society Archive)

Barkworth also found time for the administrative end of athletic activities. By July 1914, he occupied the president position of the Hessle Swimming Club, which had been created less than two years before. Perhaps Algy came to be in charge for passing the ultimate swimming test: surviving the icy waters of the North Atlantic after the sinking of the *Titanic*. And although the JP never really excelled as a football player, he was elected president of the Hessle Association Football Club on 31 July 1919.[119]

He carried on with his charity work, a Barkworth family tradition, for years to come. Algy gave £25 for the Roof Restoration Fund of the Holy Trinity Church in 1917 and was one of the original directors of the

---

119. *Hull Daily Mail*, 9 July 1914, and 8 August 1919.

church's Trust, registered in 1906. Its goal was to 'preserve the Evangelical nature of the services' and it had the power to appoint the parish's vicars. Barkworth helped run the Trust for decades and had become its chairman by 1932. He was on the Board of Alderman William Cogan's Charity, an apprenticeship program for poor boys and, in September 1940, one year after the outbreak of World War II, he contributed £10 10s on behalf of the Haltemprice Fighter Plane Fund.[120]

At the beginning of 1922, Barkworth decided to retire from his post in the East Riding County Council – unfortunately, he did not give a reason to the press.[121] Maybe the combination of being a very active member of the Hull and Hessle societies and his positions as a JP and a councilman were beginning to take a toll on the 57-year-old Englishman.

In the first days of 1926, Algy found himself in a curious position – at the other side of the magistrate bench. The defendant was not Barkworth, but a middle-aged man named Christopher Dawson. He called at Tranby House to beg and later in the evening was found sleeping in a heating house on the mansion's grounds by the master himself. In the role of witness, the justice told the court he had not thought it safe to leave him there because there was a risk of asphyxiation by sulphur fumes in the shed. Algy fed the trespasser and then handed him over to the police. Dawson, who wanted to get out of the Hull area

---

120. *Yorkshire Post and Leeds Intelligencer*, 4 July 1908, and 3 October 1923; *Hull Daily Mail*, 31 December 1917, 17 October 1930, and 28 September 1940; *Leeds Mercury*, 26 September 1932.

121. *Hull Daily Mail*, 17 February 1922.

because he could not find work there, was sent back to his hometown, Manchester, by train.

Algernon heard an amusing case in October 1926. Two boys were accused of stealing some pears from an orchard and breaking a branch from the pear tree in the process. Barkworth, in the chair, ordered the young defendants to pay the cost of the damage and court expenses, after acknowledging the trouble caused by 'hordes of boys coming out into the country'. 'I have chased them myself as long as my wind lasted', Algernon revealed. One can almost picture the aging magistrate trying – and failing – to catch up with the mischievous children.[122]

Around 1921, Barkworth met Walter Garner, a man shrouded in mystery. Very little is known about him, but it is certain he eventually became one of the most important people in Algy's life. Walter was born on 16 February 1903 in Hessle, where he also grew up. The magistrate hired him to be his chauffeur and his gardener as well. In fact, employing a servant to execute multiple tasks was fairly common in the 1910s and '20s, especially in bachelors' households.[123] Garner declared he was Algy's chauffeur in the 1921 Census, when he was only 18. This shows he already started at the top at Tranby House since a chauffeur was a rather prestigious job and one of the best paid.

Garner met Mary Elizabeth Brown, a housemaid at Tranby House, around 1927, and the two were married by September of the next year. If they lived at Al-

---

122. *Hull Daily Mail*, 6 January 1926, and 6 October 1926.

123. *Hessle Yesterday*, courtesy of Justin Lowe; researcher Gareth Russell's personal correspondence with this author.

gy's mansion until then, after the wedding the couple surely moved out. Walter and Mary continued living in Hessle, at 29 Princes Avenue, and they had a daughter named Pamela in June 1933. As of late 2021, Pamela was still alive but refused several requests to be interviewed for this publication.

Algy's relationship with Walter would evolve over the years. From strictly employer and employee, they gradually became closer and in a public way. That would be almost unimaginable in those days of class rigidity, when members of the gentry did not mix socially with their staff. However, there is evidence that Barkworth and Garner were linked as a pair.

The Hull and District Canine Society organised annual competitions, divided into dozens of classes, to select the region's best specimens. Algy competed in at least four tournaments, from 1928 to 1931, each time accompanied by a 'Mr W. Garner', which can only be Walter Garner. It is unlikely he was just a casual friend of Barkworth's because the dogs who were declared winners in the shows were owned by both of them. This 'W. Garner' was never reported attending any other events in the justice's company, indicating they did not belong to the same social circle, at least not one publicly acknowledged.

The prized dogs' names were Chu Chang Lang and Chinky, who placed respectively second and third in the 'Chow-Chows, junior, dog or bitch' category in 1928. Lang would again snatch second place in the 1929 and 1930 competitions in the 'Chow-Chow, open (dog or bitch)' class. The only year when one of their dogs won a show was in 1931, with Chinky Lee placing first in the Chow-Chows division. Given the similarity between the names, Chinky and Chinky Lee are likely the same dog.[124]

Walter's only known photo dates from the late '20s or early '30s: he was photographed in front of one of Algy's cars, impeccably dressed in his chauffeur uniform. It is possible that Barkworth himself took the picture, either because he was interested in photography or due to his affection for Garner.

Not much more is known about Garner, but a lot has been said regarding his intimacy with Barkworth. Justin Lowe believes they were 'rather close' to one an-

---

124. *Hull Daily Mail*, 23 January 1928, 11 February 1929, 10 March 1930, and 9 November 1931.

*Walter Garner, Algy's chauffeur and gardener
(Reproduced with kind permission of East Riding
Archives, reference: ERALS: DDOW/2/9 [15])*

other. 'People who worked at Tranby House were all aware of the situation there, though it wasn't talked about as weren't many things in those days', he wrote to fellow researcher Gavin Bell around 2005.[125]

Although Walter had moved in with Mary after getting married, he continued to work for Algy for several years, at least until 1939. In that year's UK Register, Garner declared he worked as a private chauffeur. His wife's

---

125. Excerpt kindly provided by Gavin Bell.

Algy (seated) with an unidentified chauffeur ca. the 1910s (John Elverson Collection)

occupation was recorded as 'unpaid domestic duties' in the same census; she probably became a housewife after the wedding to take care of their place on Princes Avenue and, after 1933, also of their daughter, Pamela.

While Walter became a husband and father, there is proof that he remained very close to Barkworth throughout the '30s. But he might not have been the only male to attract Algy's attention.

CHAPTER 6

An empathetic magistrate

The 1930s saw Algy gradually growing less active. Close to 70 years of age, the Englishman continued to lead an engaged life in the Hull and Hessle communities he loved so much, but his attendance at events and meetings began to diminish. One position he still occupied as late as 1935 was that of vice-president of the Howdenshire Conservative Association's Hessle Branch.

Barkworth was also elected president of the Hull Hairdressers' Society around 1935 and of its branch, the Hull Hairdressers' Sick and Philanthropic Society, the following year. He was an unusual choice to head both associations; Algy was not a hairdresser as far as is known and would hardly ever need a haircut by that time due to being almost bald, as the photo on this page shows.

When delegates for the East and West Riding Divisional Council of Hairdressers held their annual gathering at Hull on 25 April 1935, Barkworth, as head of the Hull branch, was there to welcome them and take them to tea. During the meeting, he boasted about the 'virility' of his society.[126]

---

126. *Hull Daily Mail*, 15 March 1935, 26 April 1935, 18 March 1936, and 2 December 1936.

Algy pictured at a relative's wedding in 1914 (Justin Lowe Collection)

Algernon's work as a magistrate, however, saw no respite. Barkworth now had 30 years of experience in the position and frequently acted as chairman in hearings. Local newspapers reported that the Englishman was in charge of the court only 22 times from 1914 to 1928, but in the '30s and '40s, he would occupy the top seat on at least 103 occasions. He never got to preside a quarter session, though. In 1937, Barkworth was elected for the first time as the chairman of the Justices of the Peace, a prestigious post he would hold again several times in the following years. A new chairman was chosen annually.[127]

As mentioned previously, chairmen spoke on behalf of other magistrates, and some of their more relevant statements and comments were reported by the press. Because of this, it is possible to catch a glimpse of Algernon's demeanour in court and what his views as a JP were.

---

127. Helen Clark's personal correspondence with this author.

Barkworth comes across as an empathetic magistrate with a keen sense of justice, mindful that, along with judging minor offences, he was also dealing with human beings implicated in troublesome situations. Back in 1927, he considered 'too sad for words' a case of a young girl who broke up with her lover and died, possibly by suicide, after being hit by a train. Algernon said something similar in an August 1935 hearing, regarding the death of the elderly Edith Hunter, who was run over by a car. 'It is a very sad case, even more so since many of us on the Bench knew Miss Hunter very well', he grieved. Barkworth was, after all, a man very involved with Hull and Hessle societies and would have known a lot of its residents. And in 1937, when a woman was found guilty of stealing a parcel of laundry, Algernon declared, 'It is a mean thing to steal from a doorstep'.[128]

In March of the following year, the magistrate showed quite a modern way of thinking when he expressed to the court, during a case concerning an assaulted young woman, that 'girls must be protected even if they are out late at night'. The accused, Albert Cosham, was sent to prison for three months with hard labour, but Algernon wanted a longer term, considering the sentence to be 'very lenient'.[129]

Addressing the defendants, Barkworth could be firm but refined. 'What you need is a little solitude', he said to George Ashman, sentenced to 12 months in jail with hard labour over two charges of theft. Algernon also declared Ashman was a 'dangerous man'. 'The

128. *Sunday Post*, 3 July 1927; *Hull Daily Mail*, 21 August 1935, and 28 July 1937.

129. *Hull Daily Mail*, 23 March 1938.

139

poor man whose cycle you took has had to go to work on his feet since. You can't go along stealing bicycles right and left', he admonished another defendant.

Barkworth even imposed a £1 fine on a man caught stealing gravel from the side of a road. 'This is a very serious thing. It is not the amount but the principle which matters', he affirmed, summarizing his ideological methods as a Justice of the Peace.[130]

Likewise, Algernon fined a couple 15 shillings because they lied about the station from which they had boarded their train in order to pay less – a mere two pence each – for their tickets. 'This may be only a matter of pence, but the railways have suffered enough from this sort of thing', the magistrate exclaimed.[131]

Another emblematic case regarding Barkworth's behaviour as a JP happened in December 1937. 21-year-old James Henry Brown was charged with stealing engine parts and lead piping. An honest thief through and through, he asked the Bench to take into consideration that he had also stolen a bicycle. Brown then asked for another chance, but Algernon would hear none of it, considering a sentence of six months' imprisonment would do him good. 'You have had your chance, and this may bring you to your senses', he declared, sounding genuinely concerned for the defendant's rehabilitation.[132]

In a curious case, the Bench put a woman named Joan Nancy Wiles on two years probation in August

130. *Hull Daily Mail*, 06 October 1937, 24 November 1938, and 29 March 1939.

131. *Hull Daily Mail*, 24 August 1938.

132. *Hull Daily Mail*, 22 December 1937.

1942 for 'sending indecent communications through the post to her neighbours', Mr and Mrs Magson. As expected, the newspaper did not disclose the content of these letters but revealed they contained 'very serious allegations against the moral character' of the couple, adultery being heavily implied. The Magsons informed the police, and a while later Mrs Wiles was seen sending a letter to the couple. When questioned by policemen, the woman confessed her wrongdoings. She denied the allegations in the letters and blamed her actions on account of her nerves.

Mrs Wiles became agitated and cried during the case's hearing in the East Riding Court. By then, her story had changed; she justified herself by saying she wrote down what someone else had told her. But Algernon, acting as chairman on that occasion, quickly put the woman in check. 'It is no use blaming anyone else; you are the guilty person... We think you ought to apologise handsomely to Mr and Mrs Magson', he announced. Besides being placed on probation, Mrs. Wiles also had to pay the costs of the proceedings.[133]

Even though the Bench dealt with minor crimes and misdemeanours, it also had to investigate some serious allegations such as in a December 1937 case, when a man, William Heslop, was charged with drinking and driving. After being taken to the police station, the defendant denied being drunk and accused the policemen of hitting him in the face and stomach. The officers claimed they did not harm Heslop, admitting only that 'a certain amount of force' had to be used when he resisted getting into the police car and exiting it on arrival at the station.

---

133. *Hull Daily Mail*, 12 August 1942.

Despite witnesses confirming Heslop's version, Barkworth sided with the cops. 'We are satisfied that he received proper treatment at the police station', the magistrate declared. Heslop ended up being fined £10 and his license was suspended for a year. Perhaps a reason for this controversial decision by the justice can be found in a case he would judge three years later. On that occasion, a letter of complaint was read at court regarding a police officer's conduct. 'If he [George Robinson, the man who wrote the letter] makes allegations against the police, he must substantiate them', Algernon explained.[134] He might have thought Heslop's accusations lacked proof.

Barkworth showed sympathy to the accused in some cases. 'I am sorry to see you in this position, because you have served your country well. I hope you will keep clear of drink in future – we find that drink is the trouble in so many of these cases that come before us', Algernon expressed to two guardsmen charged with stealing while under the influence in September 1943. And a milkman who obtained around 3s 6d from the Ministry of Food through fraud surprisingly heard some paternal counsel from the JP. 'We are amazed that a young man like you should risk your reputation. I hope it will be a lesson to you', he wished to the accused, after having imposed him a fine of £7.[135]

There were occasional recommendations to the general population, such as when Barkworth, presiding over yet another bike theft case, pointed out the police force 'might be saved a great deal of trouble if people would only remember to lock their bicycles

---

134. *Hull Daily Mail*, 16 October 1940, and 29 December 1942.

135. *Hull Daily Mail*, 19 March 1941, and 9 September 1943.

when leaving them'. In 1939, Algernon issued a 'serious warning' to cyclists: he advised that those who did not carry red rear lamps on their bicycles would be fined.[136]

Compliments to police officers who succeeded in catching thieves or preventing crimes were not uncommon – even a 12-year-old-girl who chased a bike thief on another bicycle and reported the crime to the police was congratulated by Barkworth. When Sergeant H. Dalton was promoted to the rank of inspector, Algernon paid tribute to the 'excellent work done' by the policeman.

The magistrate also expressed sadness over the passing of a court clerk and requested a moment of silence in his honour. When a fellow JP, Colonel Wellsted, died, Barkworth stated in court his colleague had always been a good friend and a kind neighbour. 'We shall all miss you very much', the justice declared on another occasion to a retiring superintendent.[137]

Algernon worked as a JP long enough to witness considerable changes in the courts, indicative of more modern and inclusive times. It was in December 1938 that he was first reported to have shared the Bench with a woman, Mrs W. B. Mateer. She, in fact, became the first ever female magistrate to sit at the Brough Court, in the South Hunsley Division, having been sworn in as a justice four years earlier.

Mrs Mateer lived in the village of Brantingham, ten miles away from Hull, and, just like Barkworth, was very much active in her community. She was a member of the National Society for the Prevention of Cruelty to

---

136. *Hull Daily Mail*, 18 October 1939, and 13 October 1943.

137. *Hull Daily Mail*, 15 December 1920, 6 October 1937, 13 October 1937, 12 September 1940, and 13 May 1943.

Children's Hull branch committee and of the Yorkshire Home for Mothers and Babies, as well as vice-president of the Ellerker Women's Institute and honourable secretary of the Brantingham Women's Club.

The Hull area was quite the pioneer and had proudly included women on their benches since 1921, only two years after the appointment of the first female magistrate in England, Ada Summers. By 1933, there were already four women acting as JPs in Hull.[138]

Although Algernon sometimes presented progressive lines of thought, we must bear in mind that he was a conservative. And no case better represents his traditional way of thinking than an August 1941 request to open the Hessle Cinema from 5.30 to 9.45 p.m. on Sundays. The application was denied, and Barkworth, the chairman, asked if the cinema owner considered it fair to put churches in competition with cinemas.[139]

Just like so many years before, the Bench would also hear special cases related to the Second World War, fought between 1939 and 1945. Starting in the conflict's second year, several citizens would find themselves fined for showing lights from unscreened windows. 'We think this is a very bad case. No attempt had been made to black-out', lamented Algernon in a particular case of a noticeable light amid an alert. Even a vehicle owner would be fined during wartime if its headlamps, sidelights and rear lights were not properly covered.[140]

138. *Hull Daily Mail*, 1 September 1933, 28 March 1934, 9 April 1934, and 7 December 1938.

139. *Yorkshire Post and Leeds Intelligencer*, 28 August 1941.

140. *Hull Daily Mail*, 16 October 1940, 11 December 1940, and 12 March 1941.

And, as in the First World War, Hull suffered air-strikes by Germany, which had retired the cumbersome Zeppelins in favour of the faster and more efficient planes. Indeed, Hitler's Luftwaffe proved deadlier than before, and the raids killed 1,200 Hull residents and injured another 3,000. 152,000 were made homeless and 86,715 houses were damaged in the port city during these attacks. Together with London, Hull became the most heavily bombed city in the United Kingdom.

There were a few occasions when Barkworth faced more serious war-related cases. A 19-year-old gun factory employee was judged in March 1942 for revealing details about a specific armament in conversation with and in a letter to a colleague who, she claimed, was already aware of the situation. She received a £5 fine and a reprimand from Algernon. He said the magistrates were shocked 'by the way she had allowed her tongue to run away with her'. 'If the information imparted had been in any way a real secret, we should undoubtedly have sent you to prison. We are also surprised the firm are keeping you', the JP declared. And a man named Reginald Dunn was fined the enormous sum of £229 for attempting to obtain money from the War Damage Commission by false pretences.[141]

Some of the war-related cases were more poignant in nature. Ivy Davis was a 28-year-old woman and a mother of six children, whose ages ranged from eight to only three. She stood before the magistrates on 25 August 1943 after being charged with stealing apples and a vegetable marrow from the orchard of Mr Frank Bradley, a veterinary surgeon. He testified that the

---

141. *Hull Daily Mail*, 18 March 1942, and 11 November 1942.

thefts occurred almost every night and the fruit trees had been damaged as a result. Mrs Davis was seen in the orchard with a bag full of stolen apples by her side. She was in the company of two of her children, one of them being up in a tree.

Acting as chairman, Algernon pointed out she was encouraging her children to steal. The woman protested. 'I did not send him into the garden', she said. Mrs Davis' husband was a chief engineer serving in the Navy, and she had only a weekly allowance of £5 9s 6d to get by. 'Food-stealing in war-time is a serious offence', Barkworth criticised, perhaps too harshly. He and the other magistrates fined the woman £4 4s. If she could not pay the amount, the alternative was going to jail for 28 days.

Ivy then burst into tears. 'My mother can take the bairns and I will do the 28 days', she sobbed. The Bench appeared to have taken pity on Mrs Davis and allowed her to pay the fine at the rate of 10s a week, less than 10% of her weekly income.[142]

Mirroring his actions during WWI, Algy again acted more mercifully towards soldiers. A 19-year-old named Peter Norman was sentenced in February 1942 to pay a £2 fine for stealing a windscreen wiper and a driving mirror from a car. In the chair, Barkworth confided that Norman only escaped going to jail because he enlisted in the Army.[143]

His leniency became even more apparent in a February 1940 case, concerning turner William Goodall, who was found guilty of stealing a height gauge and callipers from his workplace. 'You have had a very nar-

142. *Hull Daily Mail*, 25 August 1943.

143. *Hull Daily Mail*, 25 February 1942.

row escape from going to prison, but in view of the fact that your services are useful to the country at the present time, and there are no previous convictions, you will be fined £5', Algernon ruled.

Goodall worked for Blackburn Aircraft Limited, a Brough-based company that built mainly naval and maritime aircraft. During World War II, the factory intensified production of a light bomber plane called Blackburn Botha and was busy repairing war-damaged apparatus and adapting nearly 4,000 American aircrafts for use by the Fleet Air Arm, one of the five fighting arms of the Royal Navy. In passing William's sentence, Barkworth must have thought that Blackburn, with such a heavy workload, could not afford to lose a single worker.[144]

Possibly to further contribute to the war effort, Algernon became a special constable in 1939. According to Michael Free, special constables were volunteer policemen. They supplemented the official police force and still exist today in England. Special constables were not remunerated but did receive expenses and usually had a slightly different uniform to distinguish themselves from regular officers.

During an October 1939 court hearing, Clarence Davies was fined 45 shillings for physically attacking a special constable. Perhaps because he was one, Algernon gave him a 'stern warning'. 'Mr Barkworth said specials must not be assaulted by people to whom they spoke. They were doing "good work", often at personal cost, and the chairman [Algernon] hinted at greater se-

---

144. *Hull Daily Mail*, 23 February 1940; *Yorkshire Evening Post*, 21 February 1940.

verity in treatment of these cases in future', reported the *Hull Daily Mail*.[145]

The early '30s were marred by the deaths of two of Barkworth's siblings. His older brother, Edmund, passed away in February 1931, and his older sister, Evelyn, died in April 1933 after a short illness. Her obituary mentioned she would be 'much missed in the district, where she has associated herself with many religious and philanthropic objects. For some years she carried on a Mission Room in one of the poorer districts of Hessle, where she did much good work'. Her funeral took place on 2 May, and was attended by many members of Tranby House's staff, just as when farm labourers had shown up years before to mourn her father, Henry. At least nine servants were present at the ceremony, and four of them acted as pallbearers. Algernon and Violet, the two remaining siblings, were also there. With Evelyn's death, Algy became the sole Barkworth living at Tranby House.[146]

It was also in 1933 that Barkworth last spoke publicly of the *Titanic* sinking. In April of that year, some days after the twenty-first anniversary of the disaster, Algy wrote a letter to the *Hull Daily Mail* to correct a mistaken piece of information that had been printed by the newspaper. It claimed that Charles Lightoller had been the only officer to survive the tragedy. The magistrate, reading this, must have dug through his files and found the list of surviving *Titanic* officers, which included not only Lightoller (Second Officer), but also

---

145. M. G. Free's personal correspondence with this author; *Hull Daily Mail*, 25 October 1939.

146. *Hull Daily Mail*, 1 May 1933, and 2 May 1933.

Evelyn Barkworth's signed portrait
(Justin Lowe Collection)

Herbert Pitman (Third Officer), Joseph Boxhall (Fourth Officer) and Harold Lowe (Fifth Officer). 'Boxhall, anyhow, was lunching with me some months after the occurrence', added the justice, who peculiarly never identified himself as a *Titanic* survivor in his text, out of discretion or perhaps to avoid having to provide an account of the sinking to the media again.[147]

This letter reveals that, more than two decades after his near-death experience in the North Atlantic, Algy was still interested in reading what was published about the *Titanic*. This connection with the sinking manifested in other ways since he also placed a large painting of the ship in his sitting room.[148]

Another curious aspect of Barkworth's note is that he maintained an acquaintance with Officer Boxhall for at least a few months after the disaster. The lunch get-together probably came about because Boxhall was living in Hull at the time. When he embarked on the *Titanic*, the officer gave 27 Westbourne Avenue as his address. Boxhall had also been born there in 1884.

Lookout George Hogg was another survivor who originally came from Hull, but by 1912 he was living in Southampton. Four years after the sinking, Irish survivor Edward Ryan moved to Hull, where he would remain for the rest of his life. And one of Algy's Collapsible B boatmates, Third Class passenger Albert Moss, lived temporarily in the port city after the end of the Second World War in 1945. He was a Norwegian sea captain and had to complete various missions for the Allies following the conclusion of the deadly conflict.

---

147. *Hull Daily Mail*, 21 April 1933, courtesy of Michael Poirier.

148. *Hessle Yesterday*, courtesy of Justin Lowe.

CHAPTER 7

'A very eccentric old man'

Life in the late '30s at Tranby House was recorded for posterity thanks to an account penned in 1988 by Sheila Byron, who had worked at the mansion as a housemaid between 1937 and 1938, aged only 14. When she got the job, her mother, Olive, told her she did not think Tranby House was as posh as she would have liked, maybe because she had once worked as a cook for aristocrats. The noble family's lifestyle was very luxurious, with huge banquets and shooting parties. They even allowed their servants to hold an annual gathering in their ballroom. Sheila's father had been employed as a gardener by the same family, and that is how Olive met him.

Sheila's experience at Tranby House, alas, would be quite different. On her first day, she was introduced to the house's staff: Edith, the head housemaid[149]; Betty, the kitchen maid; Annie Plumb, the cook; John Henry Welton (Justin Lowe's great-grandfather), the butler; and Ronald Pickard, the page boy. 'He had the choice of either going down the mines in Derbyshire or going

---

149. She may have been Emily Shaw, who was Tranby House's housemaid in 1939 according to that year's Register. Given that this account was written more than 50 years after the narrated facts, it is possible Sheila mixed up the names.

into domestic service. I don't think he made the right choice!', Sheila wrote about Pickard.[150] Her misgivings will be discussed later on.

Sheila at first was impressed with her comfortable and attractive quarters, which boasted a carpet – a luxury item she did not have in her own house. She shared her room with Edith. It was when the girl began her chores that she realized her work would bear little resemblance to the pleasant times her parents had ex-

---

150. Sheila Byron's transcribed manuscript, page 3, courtesy of Angie Orme.

An elderly Algy is photographed reading at the front of Tranby House, ca. 1943 (Hessle Local History Society Archive)

perienced with their former employer. Since there was no running water or bathrooms on Tranby House's first floor, she had to carry water up and down the stairs every day. She was responsible for bringing hot water to the room of Rose Ann Roper, the housekeeper. Sheila also complained that there was no heating or any labour-saving devices at the mansion. The staff could not even have a radio or newspapers in the servants' hall.

Under Algy's management, Tranby House had apparently frozen in time – indifferent to the modernity that carried on outside its walls. It is no wonder that Sheila called it a 'Victorian household'. Byron remembered that, in the 18 months that she worked there, only one couple came to stay on a visit, occupying one of the mansion's guest rooms. This suggests that, as time went by, Barkworth was becoming more isolated from the society he had so much appreciated. Perhaps, as he got older and his friends began passing on, events and parties were not as entertaining as they had been in the past.

Another of Sheila's jobs was to clean Algy's study, and her recollections of those moments allow us a glimpse into his private personality:

> 'It was a fairly small room but what a lot of clutter it contained! Mr Barkworth was a survivor of the ill-fated Titanic which sank in 1912 with the loss of thousands of lives so he was very fortunate to have survived. He was a very eccentric old man aged over 70.[151] He wouldn't throw anything away, he

---

151. Indeed, Algy was 73 at the time Sheila worked there.

kept the clothes that he had been wearing when he was rescued from the sea (which I can understand), but he had a glass cupboard in which he kept all sorts of oddments all with their own labels on, such as an old bacon hook from the kitchen ceiling and a cracked china door knob'.[152]

Some of her chores did not even have a practical sense; in the summer, when the coal lumps were not being used, Sheila had to polish them to make them 'look nice'! And during spring cleaning, she had to dust each and every one of the hundreds of books from the library; she was sure that was the only time they were removed from the shelves.

---

152. Sheila Byron's transcribed manuscript, page 4, courtesy of Angie Orme.

One of Sheila's daughters, Rosalyn, remembers her mother saying how the newspapers were ironed before they were given to the master. Although today this might seem an odd and pointless task, back then it was standard practice for upper-class families. Hot irons were used to dry the ink so that the reader would not end up with black fingers.[153]

Justin Lowe argued that only Algy's servants would see the JP as eccentric. His peers in fact probably would have thought nothing of his behaviour as it was normal for the times. 'Rich people had to fill their time with pleasurable activities, and so he had a farm at the nearby village of Swanland, kept animals at Tranby House, collected cars and lots of artefacts in his home. Victorians were known for their love of artefacts and clutter as it was fashionable to cram houses full of furniture and curiosities', he wrote. However, Michael Free has described Barkworth as 'extremely grumpy'.[154]

---

153. Rosalyn Sullivan, Randy Bryan Bigham and Gregg Jasper's personal correspondence with this author.

154. Justin Lowe's personal correspondence with this author; *The September Meeting: Tranby House and the Barkworths*, page 7, Hessle Local History Society – Newsletter no. 83, courtesy of East Riding Archives.

Algy sitting in his library window at Tranby House.
This photo seems to have been taken the same day as the one reproduced on page 152 since he is dressed exactly the same in both of them. Also of note is that Barkworth's face here seems a bit gaunt and he looks thinner in general, indicating he might have been ill at the time. This is perhaps his last picture (Hessle Local History Society Archive)

Christmas of 1937 came and with it, thankfully, a day of minimum work for the Tranby House's staff (they were not given the day off). Sheila reminisced about the presents Algy gave to his servants that day and what they really meant:

> 'The kitchen maid and myself got a pair of blue checked woollen gloves. The head housemaid and cook got leather gloves but the page boy got a bike. Us [sic] young girls didn't think it was fair but suspected he was a favourite as every night he had to take Mr Barkworth's cat to see him in the study and he always stayed for about an hour presumably talking. (He never spoke a word to us if he passed us in the house.) The mystery of the bike was solved for me years later when it was discovered that Mr Barkworth was a homosexual, and it was considered page boys duty to oblige'.[155]

Sheila's mention of Algy's homosexuality was left out when her account was published as a booklet in 2015, probably to avoid offending some readers' sensibilities.[156] Sexuality can be a complex and delicate subject, but sweeping the topic under the rug is not the answer either.

---

155. Sheila Byron's transcribed manuscript, page 7, courtesy of Angie Orme.

156. Booklet kindly provided by Francis Davies and M. G. Free.

Discussing this with Angie Orme, Sheila's daughter, she provided a possible reason for her mother's finding out about the JP's sexual orientation only years later. 'I'm sure my mother wouldn't have even known what a homosexual was back in those days... it was something that was never ever discussed', she explained, also describing a meaningful encounter Sheila had with Ronald. 'My mother got in touch with the pantry boy [sic] years later, and he told her that Algernon asked him to take the cat to his bedroom [sic] so he could stroke it. Of course he wasn't interested in the cat, but the pantry boy told my mother he didn't report it because his other alternative to working in the big house as a servant was to go down the mines and he was afraid of the dark! So he endured it as he knew if he told his parents he would be sent down the mines!'[157]

So, what exactly happened behind the study's doors? Nobody knows. Nonetheless, the page boy's behaviour of ignoring other staff members as he was going to or leaving the room suggests he might have been embarrassed about what was going on. It could have been something totally innocent; Barkworth at that point of his life was becoming more reclusive and might have needed someone with whom to talk. The conversations might have seemed boring to Ronald and, as Sheila said, he had to comply.

However, according to Angie, Ronald could have reported whatever happened in there. If any sexual acts did happen, they would have been illicit. At 15, he was one year short of the minimum age of

---

157. Angie Orme's personal correspondence with this author.

consent at the time. Also, 'gross indecency between males' was a crime in the United Kingdom then and homosexuality would not be legalized until 1967. Coincidentally, the man who had encouraged the Parliament to pass the Act that raised the age of consent from 13 to 16 years and criminalized homosexual acts was none other than the journalist William Stead, who crossed paths with Barkworth during the last hours the *Titanic* was afloat.

Unfortunately, we do not have enough evidence to pinpoint where the truth lies. So, there is still room for interpretation on the matter; whatever happened, all that can be said is it did not sit well with Ronald.

It is possible Pickard was gay or bisexual himself or beginning to explore his sexuality, given what is known about him as an adult. "He was a bachelor... I never saw him with a lady friend on his visits to us or when we went to Newark. It was illegal then to be gay so relationships were secret", recalled one of his nieces, Jan Cotterill.

Jan also revealed why mining had been considered a potential field of employment for him. 'He [Ronald] was the youngest of the family, and I think their mother died giving birth to him. Their father was a miner and some of the older ones were born in South Africa, where he worked in the goldmines... He came back to the UK to work in the coal mines. All his sons except Ron worked as miners. His older sister, Edith, had to look after their father and youngest brothers and was particularly close to Ron', said Jan. This interesting titbit implies that Ronald, having seen how laborious the mining business was through his father and older brothers' experience, decided he wanted something else for himself. After working for Barkworth, he joined the Army in 1947 and served in the Middle East. Ronald died in 1982, age 60, of lung cancer. He did not have children.[158]

---

158. Jan Cotterill's personal correspondence with this author; Unknown Newspaper, courtesy of Jan Cotterill.

Members of the Tranby House staff in the 1930s. John Henry Welton, the butler, is seated at far right. The boy in the same row is probably Ronald Pickard. There's also a dog in the picture, which could have belonged to Algy (Justin Lowe Collection)

Ronald Pickard later in life. He looks very much like the boy in the photo on the previous page (Courtesy of Jan Cotterill)

Sheila's story confirms Algy stood by the promise he made publicly in 1912 and kept the clothing he was wearing when the *Titanic* sank. They were comprised of a sea-stained shirt and the fur coat which helped him stay afloat that morning in the frigid waters. Writer Brian Edwards, the magistrate's great nephew, stated that the shirt was stored in a glass case, but the priceless memento was ruined in the '20s by Barkworth's niece Dorothy after she used it to clean her motorcycle and sidecar 'from vindictiveness or mischief'. It was probably a mistake on her part because she and Algy were close.

The fur coat, on the other hand, remained with Barkworth until his death. Afterwards, it was inherited by his nephew Eric, son of Edmund and his second wife, Ellen. When Eric emigrated to Australia with his wife, Lyn, and his mother, the coat was cut down to make Ellen a cape for the cooler evenings. It eventually passed to Lyn. She lived in a provincial town in the Australian state of Queensland, where the historical item is still likely to be.[159]

---

159. Edwards, Brian, *A Swim for Dear Life – The True Story of a Titanic Survivor,* page 20. Courtesy of Bruce Robinson.

*Rose Ann Roper's portrait (Justin Lowe Collection);
the housekeeper was also photographed sitting in
the library window, just like Algy was in a photo
reproduced previously in this chapter (Hessle Local
History Society Archive)*

The account penned by Sheila Byron also disclosed how intimate the relationship was between Algy and Rose Ann Roper; the maid witnessed them having breakfast together, something unusual at the time since Roper was a member of Barkworth's staff. Miss Roper had been his mother's companion, and his sister Evelyn's after the matriarch's death in 1915. It is worth noting that secretaries or companions were not the same as maids, so she was already above a mere household servant. Because of that, she may have already been welcomed at the breakfast table for a long time, which would have allowed her to forge a lasting bond with Algy. Another possibility is that he and Roper had grown closer since Evelyn's death.[160]

160. Randy Bryan Bigham's personal correspondence with this author.

In the '30s, she occupied the position of house-keeper for the Tranby House estate at Barkworth's request, but he considered her a member of the Barkworth family. Indeed, in several adverts Algy published in newspapers looking for new servants in the '40s, he described that they would tend to the needs of a family of two. Roper was the second member.

Her elevated status came with privileges, such as better sleeping quarters. Rose Ann did not bunk in the attic with the other servants but in a bedroom right next to Barkworth's. Her room was smaller than his, of course, but it had a privileged view, right above the mansion's main doorway.

On Sundays, Algy, Roper and the rest of his staff went to All Saints' Church in Hessle, 1.6 miles away from Tranby House, an occasion Byron begrudgingly remembered. 'On the Sundays that I didn't go home, I had to go to church and had to sit in the Barkworth's servants' pew. It was a very long walk to church and no matter what the weather we still walked, very often passed by Miss Roper in the Rolls Royce with never a sideways glance', she wrote.[161]

Sheila left Tranby House in 1938 as there was rumour of a war coming and she was afraid Hull would be bombed. She chose to get a job closer to her family, who lived in the village of Welton, about five miles from Hessle. 'Thank Goodness, I'll never set foot in that house again' were Sheila's parting words from Tranby House. The girl thought her following job, also as a

---

161. Justin Lowe's personal correspondence with this author; Sheila Byron's transcribed manuscript, page 7, courtesy of Angie Orme.

maid, felt like 'sheer bliss' compared to the 'prison like conditions' she had to endure in the mansion.[162]

She was not the only one to suffer. Despite being known for a fastidious approach to work and maintaining the etiquette of the house, the butler, John Henry

162. Sheila Byron's transcribed manuscript, page 8, courtesy of Angie Orme.

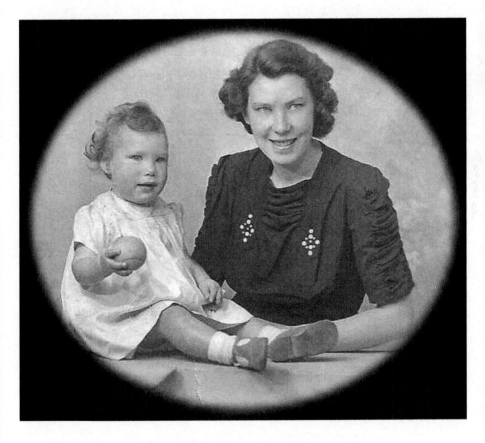

Sheila Byron with her daughter Angie
(Justin Lowe Collection)

Welton, was also given a hard time by the Barkworths, according to Welton's great-grandson, Justin Lowe. Welton opted not to live at Tranby House, unlike other servants, and that likely irritated the family. 'I don't know what the occasion was, but a lot of the staff were given gold watches and things and he didn't get anything. He was not respected for living away from them, but he had his own family to look after', Justin said. John may have been friends with Miss Roper, though, because she gave him a little prayer book, which is in Lowe's possession to this day.[163]

Even occasional workers were not exempt from Algy's strictness, as Rob Sherwood's account reveals. He was often at Tranby House to mow the mansion's large lawns in the 1940s. His memories are also valuable because they suggest the master of the house by then seemed more antisocial than ever before, preferring the company of animals instead of his peers':

> '...he never seemed to be in the house, he had a den in one of the stables, a roaring fire, and sat in there keeping an eye on people like myself who were working there. There was a dog cemetery in the grounds and I was once looking at the headstones and he came out of his lair and told me to get on with my work, I always thought he seemed to be a bit grumpy but I was

163. Free, M. G., *The House of Barkworth*, page 3, Hessle Local History Society, 2016 (unpublished); Justin Lowe's interview and personal correspondence with this author.

told that he was a survivor of the Ti-
tanic disaster in 1912, maybe the horror
of that had affected him. I never ever
saw a Mrs Barkworth and the big house
only seemed to be used by the servants.
The large house had beautiful well kept
grounds and I often wondered what it
was like to live in a mansion like that'.[164]

What Algy lacked in consideration for his em-
ployees, he made up in affection for his family, especially his beloved niece, Dorothy. Two of his letters to her survive to this day,[165] and they show how
fond Algy and Dorothy were of one another. In these
private documents, Barkworth displayed a softer,
kinder side to his personality that he did not share
with members of his staff – with the exceptions of
Miss Roper and Walter Garner.

For instance, the two messages begin with a
tender 'My dear Dorothy' greeting, and both thank her
for little gifts she gave to Barkworth. 'I was very pleased
with the very nice little pencil you so kindly sent me
for Christmas, it goes in my pocket and is not too big,
I use it every day, and like it very much. Also it was so
kind of you to send the Cream which we much enjoyed,
it is shameful of me to have forgotten to write about
it before', he wrote on 14 January 1938. The Christmas
he mentioned is the same at which he gave Ronald a
bike. In previous correspondence, Dorothy must have

---

164. *Hessle and its People*, 2007. In Free, M. G., *Algernon Henry Barkworth*, page 3 (unpublished).

165. Courtesy of John Elverson and M. G. Free.

mentioned that she had a sore throat because, in the same letter, the justice suggested she should gargle with a mild antiseptic called TCP, which he thought was 'very good, if very nasty'.

The rest of the letter is dedicated to complaints about the weather ('lots of rain and sometimes very cold') and commodity prices such as coal as well as some comments about Dorothy's siblings, Henry and Clara (nicknamed 'Betty'). Algy wrote that Henry went to 'T Wells' (a probable mention to the town of Royal Tunbridge Wells in Kent) and that he had written to Betty, sending her Christmas cards, but she had not yet sent a reply. No wonder Dorothy became his favourite niece. 'Hope that you will feel better, and with my love, your affectionate Uncle', finishes Barkworth.

This caring tone is replicated in the second surviving letter, from 2 May of the same year. Algy said he hoped Dorothy was well after her holiday and again thanked her for having sent him cream from the seaside town of Torquay, where she lived at least some months of the year.[166] Barkworth's reply was delayed because he had not been feeling well. 'I have had a rather bad attack of sciatica [leg and back pain caused by irritation and/or compression of the sciatic nerve] and have had a fortnight in bed, and altho' I am now up I cannot walk very much yet. It is really so very cold

166. In an e-mail to this author from Dorothy's nephew, researcher and writer John Elverson, he states that he believes she was living in Chelsea, London, at the time, where she owned a house or apartment, but she might have had a 'country house' in Torquay as well. Algy does mention London in his letter – 'Coals seem to go like wildfire, and I expect in London they cost a good deal more than they do here' –, so this is plausible.

and such horrid east winds and also drought that it makes it very difficult to get over anything', he lamented. Ever the rural man, the JP also worried about lost corn crops in Dorset.

However, Algy's writing went from glum to light-hearted in a snap, and he showed some sense of humour in the form of mockery and sarcasm. 'I think that's a silly looking picture that the Academy people wouldn't hang, the man looks as if he was slipping off his chair onto the floor, and such an ugly man at that. Some of the others are [h]orrid smudges of color [sic]. But of course I am I suppose a heathen or regarded so by the Artistic people with a big A', he wrote, apparently showing some discontent with the local artistic community, of which we have no other evidence.

The January and May letters also prove that Barkworth maintained a warm relationship with his chauffeur/gardener, Walter Garner, after 1931, when they last participated together in the Hull and District Canine Society shows. This lasted at least until the late '30s. Algy writes about Garner in a very telling, sentimental manner as seen in the January letter:

> *'I am very sorry to have to tell you that poor Walter has developed T. B. [tuberculosis], and has been in bed for some weeks, it's a great blow to me after all the time we have been together, I knew he wasn't looking at all as he should for over a year and begged him to go and be overhauled, but no, he always refused, and latterly had got terribly thin, so one day I phoned Dr Milli-*

*gan who sent a swab up, and the result
was to confirm my fears'*

After typewriting his letter, Barkworth added by
hand what looks like a last-minute comment about Walter's situation: 'I wouldn't mention it to Betty about Walter, as she was here so recently and they sat in front of the
car with him, not that there could be any danger in that'.[167]
Obviously, the magistrate wished to prevent Dorothy's
sister from worrying about having contracted tuberculosis. And he was right; although the malady is contagious,
it's not that easy to catch and Betty would not have been
infected with TB by merely sitting next to Walter.

Algy mentions Garner's predicament again in
the May correspondence as well as sharing one of his
housekeeper's wishes. '...poor Roper wants a change
badly as we havnt [sic] left the place since we came
home last June. And owing to poor Walter's state I can't
go on my usual Motor trip', he wrote.

The letters and other pieces of evidence presented
in this book indicate that Barkworth was gay and that
he and Walter were more than good friends. First of all,
Algy uses Walter's first name when talking about him,
which was highly uncommon at a time when servants
were addressed by their surnames.

Even Miss Roper, Barkworth's travel companion and
someone whom the magistrate considered a member of
his own family, is mentioned only by her last name –
because she was his housekeeper. Therefore, it can be
deduced that Roper was not as close to Algy as Walter.

Barkworth also wrote that he and Walter were

---

167. Transcription by M. G. Free.

'together', which is very odd phrasing to describe a master-servant relationship. Throughout the course of more than a year, Algy worried for Garner's health and even arranged for a doctor to examine him. Also, considering how he regarded the rest of his staff, all evidence points to there being more going on between the pair than meets the eye.

Indeed, the living Barkworth clan confirms the justice was gay. One of these family members is Paul Barkworth, who is Algernon's third cousin (Paul's grandfather, Harold, was Algy's first cousin). 'Yes, there was always talk of his sexuality in the family over the years, but in keeping with the mores of the time, [it] was not discussed publicly', he explained.[168]

Barkworth's sexual orientation appears to have been known even by Hessle residents. Justin Lowe remembered that his older relatives talked about Algy and Walter having an affair. Even the JP's suspiciously fancy Christmas present to Ronald did not go unnoticed by the population of the area. 'The notion was he was entwined [with Walter]', explained Justin. Sheila Byron's manuscript possibly alludes to this, since she stated 'it was discovered that Mr Barkworth was a homosexual' years after she had worked for him rather than writing 'I discovered'.[169]

Paul and Justin's statements and Sheila's account point out that perhaps Algy's homosexuality was an open secret, and people just did not talk about it be-

---

168. Paul Barkworth's personal correspondence with this author.

169. Justin Lowe's personal correspondence with this author; Sheila Byron's transcribed manuscript, page 7, courtesy of Angie Orme.

cause of his social position in the community and because the subject was still taboo at the time. Regarding Barkworth himself, he did not seem to mind candidly discussing his feelings for Walter with his family at least, as his letters to Dorothy prove.

Unfortunately, Walter did not recover and eventually succumbed to his illness. He died on 23 October 1943, aged only 40. His death certificate states the primary cause of death was toxaemia (blood poisoning by toxins from a local bacterial infection), with pulmonary tuberculosis being secondary. Mary, his wife, was with him when he passed away. Despite his possible romantic involvement with Algy, Walter appears to have been a dedicated family man; his obituary described him as the 'dearly loved husband of Mary' and 'dear daddy of Pamela', who was a mere 10-year-old child at the time[170].

His effects mysteriously amounted to £676 19s 4d, a great sum for a young labourer back then. How did Walter acquire such a fortune in so little time? It almost certainly did not come from his kin because he was born into a humble family. Garner's father, Charles, had been a coachman and a worker at a gasworks factory and died fairly young at 52 in 1922. His wife, Annie, was a housewife. His two brothers, Charles William and Frank, were also members of the working class. It is likely that the money came from Algy, strengthening the possibility the two of them had been lovers.

As the letters to Dorothy suggest, the justice's health was beginning to falter by the late 1930s. This is substantiated not only by the photos of Barkworth at

---

170. Unknown Newspaper, 1943, courtesy of Stephen Hasnip.

the beginning of this chapter, but also an experience related by Paul Barkworth. 'His [Algy's] great-nephew John, himself a young boy at the time, was introduced to Algie [sic][171] as the famous survivor of the *Titanic*. Algie was now an old man with failing heart circulation and like many elderly people, his hands felt cold to the touch. John noticed this when he shook Algie's hand and said that 'it was as if the chill of the North Atlantic had never left him!'', Paul wrote[172]. This anecdote also shows that later in life Algy was still recognized and presented as a *Titanic* survivor in family circles despite not talking publicly of the sinking since 1933.

On the East Riding Court's session of 17 May 1944, it was announced that Barkworth had resigned as a Justice of the Peace and subsequently from his post as chairman of the magistrates. Although Algernon had been occupying the topmost position in the South Hunsley Petty Sessional Division, it is possible that he never judged a single case that year; the press did not report his presence at any hearings after November 1943.

The president of the Bench, E. C. Stow, explained that Barkworth stood down because of health problems and wished him a fast recovery on behalf of the other magistrates. 'He is a gentleman, if ever there was one – a type which is fast dying out, and his services have been of the greatest possible worth to the East Riding Bench', commended Stow, followed by compliments

---

171. As stated previously, Algernon's family nickname was 'Algy'. His letters to Dorothy were signed using this spelling.

172. Paul Barkworth's personal correspondence with this author.

from other justices, solicitors and policemen.[173] Algernon was clearly a well-liked man among his peers.

His resignation was the subject of a short news story in the *Hull Daily Mail* the following day. He is described as having been interested in public life ever since he was a young man, but preferred to do his work discreetly, distributing goods to the poor 'without the world knowing it'. Algy declared – although no quotes were provided in the text – that he had never been a 'drum-beater'. 'Now aged 80, and a bachelor, he is proud of the fact that his forebears have been established in Hessle for something like 200 years', said the piece. Perhaps Barkworth was exaggerating, mistaken or was not interviewed at all because his family had settled down in Hessle in 1806, when Tranby House was built, less than 140 years before the story graced the pages of the *Daily Mail*. The paper did not even get Algy's age right – he was still two weeks shy of his 80th birthday.

Nevertheless, the reporter did correctly recall some factual episodes of his life, such as his *Titanic* survival as well as his presence on the East Riding Bench and County Council. 'His travels took him to all parts of the world, and the many contacts thus made gave him deep understanding of the human nature, qualities he brought to bear in his work as a magistrate. Outside the court he was always a courteous and helpful man', continued the piece, concluding that Barkworth would now be quite happy to tend to his garden and farming interests.[174]

But Algy's life as a retired man would not be as

173. *Hull Daily Mail*, 17 May 1944.

174. *Hull Daily Mail*, 18 May 1944.

Algy (in a ca. 1905 image) posing in his garden, to which he would dedicate himself after retiring from the Bench (Justin Lowe Collection)

peaceful as described by the *Daily Mail*. The English-man had his health to look after, and there's a good chance he was facing some trouble at his mansion as well. Barkworth's adverts seeking servants for Tranby House became frequent in the '40s, possibly because his demanding attitude discouraged people from working there over a long period of time. Another explanation is that the old world of country house living, with many servants, was coming to an end. It had flourished in Algy's youth through Edwardian times but by the 1940s his lifestyle was not that of most people, even among the very wealthy.[175]

In the past decades, Barkworth had only once used the local newspapers for hiring. That was in 1920, when he was looking for a 'smart respectable man or youth' to work on his Swanland farm. But starting in 1941, there were at least nine occasions when he placed adverts offering jobs at his mansion.The first of these, dated 30 May, offered the position of manservant who would be exempt from performing 'butler's duties'.[176] It can be deduced that, as tough as the times were for John Henry Welton at Tranby House, he was still working there at that time. This is corroborated by the 1939 UK Register, in which Welton declared that he worked as a private butler.

By 1944, perhaps word got out that it would have been better to stay unemployed than to work for Algy. Between August and December, Barkworth placed several advertisements trying to hire a housemaid but ap-

---

175. Randy Bryan Bigham's personal correspondence with this author.

176. *Yorkshire Post and Leeds Intelligencer*, 30 May 1941.

parently did not succeed. On 16 November, the English-man began looking for a cook as well as a housemaid and tried to up the ante, specifying that he was willing to pay 'good wages to suitable persons'.[177] One month and a half later, the advert Algy placed in the paper now said that he wanted only one woman to act as cook and housemaid, but still offered 'good wages' for the individual brave enough to fill the position.[178]

Again, Barkworth's temperament might have been only one of the reasons behind his struggle to find a woman servant. A maid or a cook was no longer a po-sition most married women could handle; they had to juggle a husband and children, which would have pre-vented their availability. These jobs in Edwardian days were often filled by single women, who had less oppor-tunities then than they had in the 1940s.[179] All around him, life as Algy knew it was changing fast, and he did not seem either ready or willing to do the same.

On 30 December 1944, he placed his last advert in the papers. Barkworth was still looking for a cook/housemaid, offering again 'good wages to suitable person'.[180] The position was probably never filled, but if it was, the woman hired did not work at the mansion for long – that is because Algy died at Tranby House on 7 January 1945, age 80, from toxaemia, the same condition that had taken Walter Garner. Contributing

177. *Hull Daily Mail*, 16 November 1944.

178. *Yorkshire Post and Leeds Intelligencer*, 29 December 1944.

179. Randy Bryan Bigham's personal correspondence with this author.

180. *Yorkshire Post and Leeds Intelligencer*, 30 December 1944.

causes of death were bronchorrhea, chronic bronchitis and emphysema. As she had always been since the '30s, Rose Roper was by his side in the end. He was described as a 'person of independent means' on his death certificate, summarizing a life lived in opulence and luxury.

Epilogue

At the time of his passing, Algy's fortune amounted to £83,968 gross (about £3,700,000 currently), with net personal estate of £74,494. £3,000 of that amount would go to his housekeeper-turned-family member, Rose Roper. In his will, he considered the money to be a 'slight acknowledgement of her services' to his family and himself. He also left £500 to the Holy Trinity Church, £100 to Henry Thompson, who had been a bailiff at his farm, and £100 to his former chauffeur, Leonard Crawford.[181] One can only imagine how much he would have left Garner if he were still alive.

'He was in heart and action one of nature's gentlemen – one of a type which is fast dying out, and we, together with his relatives, mourn his passing. Although Mr Barkworth had not been an active member of this Court since last May, we still looked upon him as one of us', lamented E. C. Stow, Algernon's successor as chairman of the magistrates, during a session which took place three days after his passing. On behalf of the solicitors practising in the Court, T. L. Witty said that they would always remember the late JP's courtesy with gratitude, as well as his kindness to the younger members of the profession in particular. Barkworth also received a tribute by Inspector C. A. Bennett, representing the police force.[182]

---

181. *Derby Daily Telegraph*, 25 July 1945.

182. *Hull Daily Mail*, 10 January 1945.

A lot of what Algy had gathered during his life-time wound up being sold at auction. In just four days in July 1945, the contents of the garden and outdoor areas, kitchen, bedroom, hall, library, morning room, drawing room and dining room were all gone. Even one of his beloved cars, a 1938 Vauxhall, was sold off. In less than a week, the remnants of Barkworth's life were spread to the winds.

Originally, Tranby House was to be offered to the general public as well, but that changed when the Department of Education of the East Riding County Council became interested in acquiring it around March of that year. The firm that was going to sell the mansion took it out of its catalogue after that. Algy's executors, Miss Roper and his niece Dorothy (chosen by Barkworth himself in his will), sold the house to the County Council of the Administrative County of York (East Riding) for £6,400.

By 1947, the mansion had been converted into a secondary school, which started receiving students on 22 September of that same year and still exists today. It is called Hessle High School & Sixth Form College or the Hessle Academy. Tranby House was listed in 1967 as a Grade II building, ensuring that its heritage and architecture will be preserved. A building is listed when it is considered of special architectural or historical interest or of national importance. Such buildings are legally protected from being demolished, extended or altered significantly without permission. Michael Free

Leonard Crawford received £100 from
Algernon's will (Justin Lowe Collection)

explains that it was quite common for mansions like Tranby House to be converted into schools in England. 'Old large houses such as Tranby had several large rooms which could be used as classrooms and smaller rooms for offices', he said. According to his research, all of Tranby House's outbuildings are now gone. Out of all the rooms, only the former drawing room, on the ground floor, remains largely intact. The dining room and the library have been converted into offices.[183]

'The house is in excellent condition', added Sarah Greenley, operations manager at The Hessle Academy. 'It still has the sash windows, high skirtings, ornate covings and the original staircase. There is a cellar and an attic, all giving glimpses of the building's former glory. The driveway, where Algernon proudly drove his motor vehicles up and down, is still in position – snaking its way through the school grounds to the pillared entrance to Tranby House'.[184] A much larger school was built on the property's grounds in 2016 and used as a secondary school for students aged 11 to 16. The mansion was then converted into a Sixth Form Centre, reserved for teenagers and young adults.

---

183. M. G. Free's personal correspondence with this author; Free, M. G., *The House of Barkworth*, page 2, Hessle Local History Society, 2016 (unpublished).

184. Sarah Greenley's personal correspondence with this author.

Tranby House was reopened in 1947 as a high school. Here it is in the 1950s... (Justin Lowe Collection)

...and today; the large building is used as a secondary school (Courtesy of Sarah Greenley / The Hessle Academy)

What is a Sixth Form College?

According to Sarah Greenley, operations manager at The Hessle Academy, children in England do not finish formal education until age 18. They must remain in either education, training or employment through an apprenticeship until they achieve that age. A sixth form college is for students who are 16-18 (the years between secondary education and university). They study three or four subjects before deciding on a major on which to concentrate at university or to obtain employment.

'A Sixth Form College gives the student more independence, they have more free time to study according to their needs, they can express themselves through clothes rather than being restricted to uniform. Students of Hessle High School can decide to stay at Hessle Sixth Form (Tranby House is a dedicated Sixth Form Centre) in an environment they are familiar with whilst studying locally to their homes', explained Greenley in an e-mail to this author.

For decades, the school maintained Barkworth's pet cemetery, and many students remember passing by it in the side garden, to the west of the house. According to Justin Lowe, the graveyard is thought to have been either totally lost or buried when some earthworks took place in 2016 – probably connected with the construction of the secondary school.

Greenley declared to have never seen this cemetery even back when she was a student at Hessle High in the 1980s. Alumni contacted by this author said that there were two to four dogs and even a horse buried in the school grounds, their graves bearing little headstones. Four of the animals were called Fly, Mick, Bess and Sky.[185]

Their master was buried elsewhere. Algy is resting beside his sister Evelyn in Mill Lane Cemetery in the village of Kirk Ella, situated just outside Hull. Their gravestone quotes a Biblical verse from the Book of Revelation: 'They shall walk with me in white for they are worthy'. Barkworth's privilege, it seems, did not abandon him even in death.

---

185. *Hessle High School - All Year Groups, Friends & Staff* Facebook Group, 21 April 2021; Justin Lowe's personal correspondence with this author; *Hessle High School Old Gits* Facebook Group, 21 April 2021; *Hessle Photos and History* Facebook Group, 18 April 2021; Lesley Anthony's personal correspondence with this author.

Algy and Evelyn's grave
(Hessle Local History Society Archive)

Acknowledgments

No book can be a one-person job, and this one is no different. In order to pull off the task of narrating Algy's long life in an accurate manner, I had to rely on other people's help. Without them, this work would not have seen the light of day.

First and foremost, I have to recognize Justin Lowe and Michael Free's major contributions. They not only supplied a lot of material on Barkworth, including photos, but discussed him at length with me, giving this author the necessary background to write his story. Additionally, I must thank my friends Randy Bryan Bigham, Gregg Jasper, Jean Carlos Scuissiato and Brandon Whited for helping me in several ways, especially in proofreading this work (a task to which Lowe and Free also contributed). I have had interesting conversations regarding Algy with John Elverson, Helen Clark, Gavin Bell, Michael Poirier, Gareth Russell, Rich Edwards, Bill Barkworth, Bruce Robinson, Gael Barkworth and Francis Davies. Thank you so much for your help.

I also must extend my gratitude to people who either have rooted for the success of this enterprise or have provided very useful information on the world surrounding Barkworth. They are: Günter Bäbler, Victor Vila, Ioannis Georgiou, Jordan Tancevski (four dear friends of mine), Bruce Beveridge, Angie Orme, Anthony Cunningham, Martin Gee, Jan Cotterill, Sarah Greenley,

Rosalyn Sullivan, Rachel Byron-Chappel, Libby Byron, Beck Price, Mark Bateman, Stephen Eccles, Lesley Anthony, Philip Hind, Stephen Hasnip, Daniel Milford-Cottam, Jeff Mcnab, Allan Fellowes, Janet Kemp Jowett, John Holmes, Sue Bailey, Dianne Bush, Elaine Wright, Shelley Ann Saddington, Susanne Störmer, Meg Sencil, Sue Recks and Barbara Cooke Mills.

Last but not least, a special shoutout to my family and friends, who have supported me every step of the way. I deeply apologize if my bad memory has prevented me from mentioning someone.

This book is also your accomplishment.

Sources

Books and Articles

BEHE, George. **Voices from Carpathia** - Rescuing RMS *Titanic*. Stroud: The History Press, 2015.

_____. **'Those Brave Fellows'** – The Last Hours of the *Titanic*'s Band. George Behe, 2020.

BEVERIDGE, Bruce; ANDREWS, Scott; HALL, Steve; KLISTORNER, Daniel; BRAUNSCHWEIGER, Art. **Titanic – The Ship Magnificent**. Volume I. Stroud: The History Press, 2012.

BYRON, Sheila. **Below Stairs at Tranby House – Memories of Domestic Service**. AWAKE U3A, 2015. Courtesy of Francis Davies and M G Free.

CORNWALL, Thomas. **Titanic – The John B "Jack" Thayer Jr Chronicles**. 2019.

DALBY, Shirley; BROOKS, Derek; HOLMES, John. **A New History of Swanland – The School and the Twentieth Century**. Swanland: Swanland Village History Group, 2003. Courtesy of Justin Lowe.

EDWARDS, Brian. **A Swim for Dear Life – The True Story of a Titanic Survivor**. Selsdon: Gordons Publishing, 1998. Courtesy of Bruce Robinson.

FITCH, Tad; LAYTON, J. Kent; WORMSTEDT, Bill. **On A Sea of Glass: The Life & Loss of the RMS Titanic**. Stroud: Amberley, 2013.

GRACIE, Archibald; THAYER, John B. **Titanic: A Survivor's Story & The Sinking of the S. S. Titanic**. 3. ed. Chicago: Academy Chicago Publishers, 2010.

HALPERN, Samuel et al. **Report into the Loss of the SS Titanic**. Stroud: The History Press, 2016.

HALPERN, Samuel. **Strangers on the Horizon: Titanic and Californian – A Forensic Approach**. Samuel Halpern, 2019.

HARPER, James T. **Dr. Frank Blackmarr's Remarkable Scrapbook – A Carpathia Passenger's Collection**. The Titanic Commutator, number 143, 1998. Pages 20-33. Courtesy of Gregg Jasper.

HYSLOP, Donald; FORSYTH, Alastair; JEMIMA, Sheila. Titanic Voices. Southampton: Southampton City Council, 2006.

LIGHTOLLER, Charles Herbert. **Titanic and Other Ships**. Middletown, 2016.

MARSHALL, Logan. **Sinking of the Titanic and Great Sea Disasters**. 1912.

MOWBRAY, Jay Henry. **Sinking of the Titanic: Thrilling Stories Told By Survivors**. Harrisburg: The Minter Company, 1912.

SEBAK, Per Kristian. **Titanic – 31 Norwegian Destinies**. Oslo: Genesis Forlag, 1998.

The Barkworth family and Tranby House, Hessle. Hessle Local History Society, Newsletter no. 75, March 2014. Courtesy of M. G. Free.

The March meeting: An Impromptu Talk on Tranby

House. Hessle Local History Society, Newsletter no. 82, July 2016. Courtesy of M. G. Free.

The September meeting: Tranby House and the Barkworths. Hessle History Society, Newsletter no.83, November 2016, p 10-12. Courtesy of East Riding Archives.

Guide / Report

DAWSON, Victoria; JOHNSTON, Helen; SHORE, Heather. **Our Criminal Ancestors – Sources for Researching Your Criminal Past**. Hull: Arts and Humanities Research Council, 2018.

Planning Heritage Ltd. **Planning Heritage: Conservation Planning Consultancy**. Bath, 2015.

Websites

https://www.encyclopedia-titanica.org/titanic-survivor/algernon-barkworth.html

https://www.encyclopedia-titanica.org/titanic-victim/charles-cresson-jones.html

https://www.encyclopedia-titanica.org/titanic-victim/arthur-gee.html

http://www.titanicology.com/Titanica/GulfStreamGo.htm

http://daytoninmanhattan.blogspot.com/2020/04/the-hotel-breslin-ace-hotel-broadway.html

https://www.nps.gov/mima/north-bridge-questions.htm

https://wormstedt.com/titanic/lifeboats/occupancy.pdf

https://www.etoncollege.com/about-us/our-history/

https://discovery.nationalarchives.gov.uk/details/r/09897c59-1c7e-436c-9e6a-a44f36e63099

https://venn.lib.cam.ac.uk/

https://www.gov.uk/become-magistrate

https://www.magistrates-association.org.uk/About-Magistrates

https://www.webcitation.org/6DuZJAhDQ?url=http://www.leighrayment.com/commons/Hcommons4.htm

https://ww1hull.com/air-raids-on-hull1/

https://www.bbc.com/news/uk-england-humber-32917351

https://www.mylearning.org/stories/zeppelin-raids-in-the-humber-during-ww1/804?

https://www.bbc.com/news/uk-england-humber-31919031

https://www.bbc.com/news/uk-england-humber-36212234

http://news.bbc.co.uk/2/hi/uk_news/england/humber/6324301.stm

https://pt.findagrave.com/memorial/12381421/algernon-henry_wilson-barkworth

http://www.cymdeithashanesmechell.co.uk/atcs.html

https://www.encyclopedia-titanica.org/titanic-survivor/edward-ryan.html

https://www.sites.google.com/site/hesslelocalhistory-society

https://www.spine-health.com/conditions/sciatica/what-you-need-know-about-sciatica

https://mayoclinic.org/diseases-conditions/tuberculosis/symptoms-causes/syc-20351250

https://www.immigrantships.net/v6/1900v6/titanic19120418_15.html

https://www.bidwells.co.uk/what-we-think/what-does-grade-2-listed-mean/

https://www.encyclopedia-titanica.org/william-mellors.html

https://www.hrr.co.uk/about/

https://historicengland.org.uk/advice/your-home/owning-historic-property/listed-building/

http://freepages.rootsweb.com/~jray/genealogy/boulderson/emma.htm

https://sites.google.com/site/tranbyhouse/home

https://www.usinflationcalculator.com/

https://www.measuringworth.com/calculators/ppoweruk/

https://www.eastridingmuseums.co.uk/EasySiteWeb/EasySite/StyleData/culture/downloads/museums/past-exhibits/beverley-guildhall/crime-and-punishment-in-beverley.pdf

https://ourcriminalancestors.org/quarter-sessions/

https://www.britannica.com/biography/Edward-J-Smith

https://www.etoncollege.com/about-us/our-history/

http://www.atlantajuniors.com/ajra-faqs/

https://nationalmotormuseum.org.uk/ufaqs/what-was-the-first-motor-car-to-run-on-the-british-highway/

https://www.britannica.com/topic/harvest

https://theweald.org/N10.asp?ID=16734

https://edm.parliament.uk/early-day-motion/30022/centenary-of-1906-general-election

https://visitbath.co.uk/things-to-do

https://www.baesystems.com/en/heritage/brough

https://en.wikipedia.org/wiki/Demography_of_England

https://www.rrauction.com/auctions/lot-detail/344591406120322-titanic-harold-cottam-and-algernon-barkworth-2-marconigrams

https://www.nytimes.com/1996/04/21/travel/l-below-stairs-092134.html

https://www.facebook.com/photo/?fbid=10221825477722428

About the Author

Photo: Lindomar Cailton

Bruno Piola was born in Franca, in the state of São Paulo (Brazil) on 10 April 1990, 78 years to the day after the *Titanic* left Southampton on her maiden voyage. Piola has a degree in Journalism and has worked as a reporter, editor, radio announcer and press officer. Today he works as a civil servant in his hometown's Town Council.

Bruno has written articles on the *Titanic* for the Titanic International Society. He also published his first book, *Faces do Titanic* (Faces of the Titanic) in 2020, which revealed, for the first time, all the connections Brazil has to the famous ship.

Made in Brazil
Franca, SP
27 April 2022